COMPULSORY RETIREMENT- SERVICE MATTERS- SUPREME COURT'S LATEST LEADING CASE LAWS

CASE NOTES- FACTS- FINDINGS OF APEX COURT JUDGES & CITATIONS

JAYPRAKASH BANSILAL SOMANI

ISBN 979-888569071-3

Dedicated

To

All the Past & Present Judges of the Supreme Court of India.

Salute to their wisdom.

Salute to their interpretation of Law.

Salute to their elaborative judgement writing.

Contents

Contents

Preface

Dear Learned Advocates of the Trial Courts, Tribunals, Appellate Tribunals, High Courts, Supreme Court, HR Professionals, Corporates, Govt Recruitment Officers & Employees,

I am very delighted to provide you a book on 'Compulsory Retirement - Service Matters' - Supreme Court of India's Latest Leading Case Laws'.

In this book you will get...

1. Name of the Case i. e. Cause title

2.Relevant Sections discussed in the case

3.Hon'ble Judges/Coram of the case

4.Number of PDF Pages in Original Judgement of the case

5. All available Citations of the case

6. Case Note with appeal allowed/ dismissed or disposed off

7. Facts of the case

8.Hon'ble Apex Court's findings, while dismissing/allowing or disposing the appeal

9. Ratio Decidendi if any.

My special thanks to Manupatra, because of their web portal I can compile this book in well manner. I am also thankful to Notion Press to support me to publish & market this book throughout the Country. Thanks to my Juniors, Advocate Colleagues & Insolvency Professional Colleagues to support me in this venture.

Miss Devpriya Shah has helped me a lot to compile this book.

I hope this book will add some value addition in the wealth of your legal knowledge. Your positive feedbacks will boost me to compile/ write further books & negative feedbacks will improve my skills. Kindly send your valuable feedbacks by email.

Thanks with Regards,

Jayprakash B. Somani

Advocate, Supreme Court of India

Email: jaysomani64@gmail.com

Web Site:www.jayprakashsomani.com

Call: 8384051134, 9322188701, 9318381287

Acknowledgements

Printed & Published by
Notion Press
No. 8, 3rd Cross Street,
CIT Colony, Mylapore,
Chennai, Tamil Nadu- 600004

Managed by
Jayprakash Somani Advocates & Solicitors
Law Firm for Supreme Court of India
Delhi Office
257 C, Pocket 1, Mayur Vihar Phase 1, Delhi 110091.
Call 8384051134, 9322188701, 8459194576, 01141051516
Supreme Court Chamber
312, 3rd Floor, M. C. Setalvad Block, In front of 'D' Gate, Bhagwan Das Road, Supreme Court of India, New Delhi 110001
Contact: 8459194576, 9811011747
www.jayprakashsomani.com

Books are available online at

1. Notion Press: https://notionpress.com/author/jayprakash_somani
2. Amazon: https://www.amazon.in/s?k=jayprakash+somani
3. Flipkart: https://www.flipkart.com/search?q=Jayprakash%20Somani

CHAPTER ONE

National Gandhi Museum Vs. Sudhir Sharma, 2021

Hon'ble Judges/Coram:

Ajay Rastogi and Abhay Shreeniwas Oka, JJ.

Equivalent Citation: 2021LLR1040, 2021(4)SCT176(SC), MANU/SC/0705/2021

Relevant sections: Section 33 of Industrial Disputes Act, 1947

Number of pages in original Judgment: 06

Case Note:

Labour and Industrial - Misconduct - Chargesheet issued challenged - Respondent in inquiry held guilty - Penalty of compulsory Retirement imposed - Prior approval application withdrawn on the premise of not needed in such situation - Appellant in challenge directed to reinstate Respondent - By impugned judgment appeal dismissed - Hence the present appeal - Whether reinstatement as directed against the Appellant sustainable?

Brief Facts:

In the instant appeal, respondent was directed to be reinstated on the ground that penalty of compulsory retirement was not in accordance to statute and thus was a nullity. By impugned judgment, High Court had dismissed the challenge made by Appellant. Hence, the present appeal.

Held, while partly allowing the Appeal:

i. The Respondent did not raise any industrial dispute for challenging the outcome of the inquiry. The Inquiry Officer concluded that the charge of assaulting the Assistant Director of the Appellant was proved against the

Respondent.

ii. Considering the aims and object of the Appellant and the serious nature of misconduct proved against the Respondent, instead of granting reinstatement, by balancing the conflicting interests, appropriate compensation needs to be awarded. Moreover, considering the nature of the misconduct proved against the Respondent, the grant of reinstatement will not be in the interest of justice.

iii. The Appellant is carrying on noble activities of propagating the thoughts of the Father of Nation by using the corpus given by the Government and by utilizing donations and sale proceeds of small articles.

iv. Appeals partly allowed by setting aside the order of reinstatement of the Respondent and the order of payment of back wages to the Respondent. Appellant directed to consolidated compensation.

CHAPTER TWO

Union of India (UOI) and Ors. Vs. P. Balasubrahmanayam, 2021

Hon'ble Judges/Coram:
Sanjay Kishan Kaul and Hrishikesh Roy, JJ.

Equivalent Citation: AIR2021SC1257, 2021(2)BLJ402, 2021(2)ESC362(SC), [2021(169)FLR128], 2021(2)J.L.J.R.6, 2021(2)PLJR175, (2021)5SCC662, 2021(2)SCT90(SC), 2021(2)SLJ1(SC), 2021(3)SLR1(SC), (2021)2UPLBEC1282, MANU/SC/0146/2021

Relevant sections: Rule14 of the Central Civil Services (Classification, Control and Appeal) Rules, 1965

Number of pages in original Judgment: 07

Case Note:

Service - Violation of duties - Disciplinary Proceedings - Rule14 of the Central Civil Services (Classification, Control and Appeal) Rules, 1965 (1965 Rules) - Central Civil Services (Conduct) Rules, 1964 - Charge Memo - Respondent contended that mandatory advice of Central Vigilance Officer (CVO) as per relevant departmental circular dated 18.01.2005(Circular) not obtained - Tribunal and High Court in appeal opined that Circular did not mandate any prior approval, causing it to be challenged before SLP - Meanwhile, the departmental proceeding held that no charges of bribery made out against the Respondent but those relating to procedural lapses were proved - Respondent inflicted with punishment of compulsory retirement - Tribunal held that since the bribery charges were not proved, case of the Respondent notprejudiced by not referring it to CVO – Punishment of compulsory retirement held to be unduly harsh and disproportionate - In Writ authorities were directed to reinstate

Respondent - Whether punishment as inflicted proportionate to charges invoked or liable to be set aside?

Brief Facts:

The present service matter concerns with disciplinary proceedings assailed on the ground that since allegations included charges of bribery, approval of Central Vigilance Officer (CVO) was mandatory. Since it was obtained, it was contended that proceedings initiated were not proper. Departmental proceeding conducted held that no charges of bribery made out but procedural lapse stood proved. The matter accordingly came up to adjudicate on the issue of adjudging correctness of proportionality of punishment inflicted.

Held, while allowing the Appeal:

i. Reliance on the Circular really does not help the case of the Respondent inter alia for the reason that once it is found that the case does not have a vigilance angle, albeit after conclusion of inquiry, no prejudice can be said to have caused to the Respondent. The only charges found proved are of procedural irregularities, over which there are concurrent findings of the relevant authorities based on certain admissions made by the Respondent himself. The proceedings have also got prolonged because at every stage the Respondent sought to challenge them in judicial forums, and that too not very successfully.
ii. There was negligence on the part of the Respondent in performing his duties. That being so, It was inappropriate for the High Court to have set aside the result of the proceedings against the Respondent by giving him a clean chit on the issue as a consequence of the Circular not being followed.
iii. Course adopted by the Tribunal was appropriate course of action, i.e., the procedural lapses having been found and the bribery allegation having been rejected the appropriate course would have been to examine only the issue of disproportionality of punishment.
iv. Judicial forums do not sit as an appellate authority to substitute their mind with the mind of the disciplinary authority insofar as the finding is concerned.
v. Direction of the Tribunal liable to be sustained.

vi. Impugned judgment of the High Court set aside and that of the Tribunal restored. Appeals allowed.

CHAPTER THREE

Rajinder Goel Vs. High Court of Punjab and Haryana and Ors., 2021

Hon'ble Judges/Coram:
U.U. Lalit and Ajay Rastogi, JJ.

Equivalent Citation: AIR2021SC3778, 2021(5)ALT13, 2021 4 AWC3644SC, 2021(5)BLJ139, 2021(3)KLJ894, 2021LabIC3611, (2021)203PLR373, (2021)9SCC88, 2021(3)SCT547(SC), 2021(3)SLJ41(SC), MANU/SC/0492/2021

Relevant sections: Article 32 of the Constitution of India, 1950

Number of pages in original Judgment: 04

Case Note:

Service - Quashing of recommendation - Compulsory Retirement - Post of Additional District and Sessions Judge - Article 32 of the Constitution of India, 1950 - Order passed by Governor of Haryana accepting the recommendation made by Full Court of the High Court sought to be quashed - Whether Petitioner entitled to relief in the given circumstances?

Brief Facts:

The Petitioner, posted as Additional District and Sessions Judge subjected to enquiry pursuant to certain complaints made against him. There were "heavy unexplained bank transactions" observed. The report was reviewed by the Administrative Committee of the High Court. Competent Authority issued order compulsorily retiring Petitioner as a measure of penalty from the membership of Haryana Superior Judicial Service. Petitioner did not accept the suggestion to take up the issue before the High Court instead. Hence the present petition.

Held, while dismissing the Petition:

i. In view of the record indicating that there were multiple transactions showing deposits and withdrawals of substantial amounts of money, it could not be said that the Full Court was not justified in taking the view that it did. No reason to take a different view in the matter.

ii. An application was preferred submitting that the Petitioner be allowed to withdraw the instant petition with further liberty to approach the High Court invoking its jurisdiction under Article 226 of the Constitution of India. Since the suggestion made by the Court was not accepted after due instructions from the Petitioner, prayer made rejected. No merit in this petition and hence rejected.

CHAPTER FOUR

Boloram Bordoloi Vs. Lakhimi Gaolia Bank and Ors., 2021

Hon'ble Judges/Coram:

Ashok Bhushan, R. Subhash Reddy and M.R. Shah, JJ.

Equivalent Citation: AIR2021SC872, 2021 2 AWC1782SC, 2021(2)BLJ203, 2021(I)CLR712, 2021(1)ESC198(SC), [2021(168)FLR646], 2021(2)J.L.J.R.41, 2021LabIC1171, 2021LLR316, 2021(2)PLJR29, (2021)3SCC806, 2021(1)SLJ612(SC), 2021(2)SLR422(SC), (2021)1UPLBEC567, MANU/SC/0057/2021

Number of pages in original Judgment: 05

Case Note:

Service - Compulsory retirement - Appellant was Manager of first Respondent-bank - On basis of certain allegations levelled against him, disciplinary proceedings were initiated and charge memo was issued - In view of reply filed by him, denying charges, Respondent-bank having not satisfied with explanation, had decided to order departmental enquiry against Appellant - Enquiry Officer, had held that all charges framed against Appellant were proved - In view of findings recorded by Enquiry Officer, Respondent-bank had proposed to inflict punishment of compulsory retirement on Appellant - Based on findings recorded in departmental enquiry, had passed order imposing punishment of compulsory retirement from service - Appellant was unsuccessful before departmental appellate authority - Appellant approached High Court before High Court - Single Judge had not interfered with order of compulsory retirement - As against order of Single Judge, Appellant had preferred Writ Appeal - Division Bench of High Court, had dismissed same by confirming order of Single Judge - Hence, present appeal - Whether impugned order of compulsory retirement was perverse.

Brief Facts:

The Appellant was the Manager of the first Respondent-bank. On the basis of certain allegations levelled against him, disciplinary proceedings were initiated and charge memo was issued. In view of the reply filed by him denying the charges, the Respondent-bank having not satisfied with the explanation, had decided to order departmental enquiry against the Appellant. The Enquiry Officer, after completing the enquiry by appreciating the oral and documentary evidence on record, had held that all the charges, framed against the Appellant were proved. In view of the findings recorded by the Enquiry Officer, the Respondent-bank had proposed to inflict the punishment of compulsory retirement on the Appellant. Based on the findings recorded in the departmental enquiry, had passed order imposing the punishment of compulsory retirement from service. The Appellant was unsuccessful before the departmental appellate authority, i.e., Board of Directors of the Bank and the appellate authority had dismissed his appeal confirming the order of the disciplinary authority. Challenging the order of the disciplinary authority imposing the punishment of compulsory retirement, as confirmed by the appellate authority, the Appellant approached the High Court. The Single Judge had not interfered with the order of compulsory retirement but at the same time had found that withholding of the service benefits including pensionary dues was illegal and issued directions for payment of such benefits to the Appellant. As against the order of the learned Single Judge, the Appellant has preferred Writ Appeal. The Division Bench of the High Court, by the impugned order, had dismissed the same by confirming the order of the Single Judge.

Held, while dismissing the appeal:

i. The Appellant was working as a Manager of the Respondent-bank. A perusal of the charges, which are held to be proved by the Enquiry Officer, reveal that he had sanctioned and disbursed loans without following the due procedure contemplated under law and also there were allegations of misappropriation, disbursing loans irregularly in some instances to (a) units without any shop/business (b) more than one loan to members of same family etc. The Enquiry Officer, after considering oral and documentary evidence on record, had held that all the charges were proved. Based on the findings recorded by Enquiry Officer, the disciplinary authority had tentatively decided to impose punishment of compulsory retirement. Disciplinary authority had issued show cause notice by enclosing a copy of the enquiry report. In response to the show cause notice, the Appellant had submitted his comments vide letter indicating that due to work pressure some operational lapses had occurred. Further he had also pleaded that if the bank had sustained any loss due to his fault, he was ready to bear such loss from his own source. After filing the response to the show cause notice, order was passed by disciplinary authority imposing punishment of compulsory retirement. After Enquiry Officer records his findings, it was always open for the disciplinary authority to arrive at tentative conclusion of proposed punishment and it could indicate to the delinquent employee by enclosing a copy of the enquiry report. Though the Appellant had argued that even before tentative conclusion was arrived at by the disciplinary authority, the enquiry report had to be served upon him, but there was no such proposition laid down in the judgment of this Court in the case of Managing Director, ECIL, Hyderabad. In the said judgment of this Court it is held that delinquent employee is entitled to a copy of the enquiry report of the enquiry officer before the disciplinary authority takes a decision on the question of guilt of the delinquent. Merely because a show cause notice is issued by indicating the proposed punishment it could not be said that disciplinary authority has taken a decision. A perusal of the show cause notice itself makes it clear that along with the show cause notice itself enquiry report was also enclosed. As such, it could not be said that the procedure prescribed under the Rules was not followed by Respondent-bank. In the case of Managing Director, ECIL, Hyderabad was not helpful to the case of the Appellant. The punishment was imposed based on the findings recorded in the enquiry report, as such, no further elaborate reasons were required to be given by the disciplinary authority. As the departmental appeal was considered by the Board of Directors in the meeting. In that view of the matter, there was no merit in the submission of the Appellant that orders impugned were devoid of reasons.

ii. Even, the last submission of the Appellant that the punishment imposed was disproportionate to the gravity of charges, also could not be accepted. The charges framed against the Appellant in the departmental enquiry were serious and grave. If we look at the response, in his letter, to the show cause notice issued by the disciplinary authority, it was clear that he had virtually admitted the charges, however, tried to explain that such lapses occurred due to work pressure. Further he went to the extent of saying-he was ready to bear the loss suffered by the bank on account of his lapses. The manager of a bank plays a vital role in managing the affairs of the bank. A bank officer/employee deals with the public money. The nature of his work demands vigilance with the in-built requirement to act carefully. If an officer/employee of the bank was allowed to act beyond his authority, the discipline of the bank will disappear. When the procedural guidelines were issued for grant of loans, officers/employees are required to follow the same meticulously and any deviation will lead to erosion of public trust on the banks. If the manager of a bank indulges in such misconduct, which is evident from the charge memo and the findings of the enquiry officer, it indicates that such charges are grave and serious. Inspite of proved misconduct on such serious charges, disciplinary authority itself was liberal in imposing the punishment of compulsory retirement. In that view of the matter, it could not be said that the punishment imposed in the disciplinary proceedings on the Appellant, was disproportionate to the gravity of charges. As such, this submission of the Appellant also could not be accepted.

CHAPTER FIVE

Canara Bank and Ors. Vs. Kameshwar Singh, 2020

Hon'ble Judges/Coram:

S. Abdul Nazeer and Sanjiv Khanna, JJ.

Equivalent Citation: AIR2020SC329, 2020(1)CGLJ325, 2020(I)CLR462, [2020(165)FLR150], 2020(1)J.L.J.R.285, 2020LabIC1856, 2020LLR120, 2020(1)PLJR329, (2020)2SCC507, (2020)1SCC(LS)371, 2020 (2) SCJ 62, 2020(1)SCT585(SC), 2020(2)SLR74(SC), (2020)1UPLBEC1, MANU/SC/0017/2020

Relevant sections: Regulation5(3) of Discipline and Appeal Regulations, 1976

Number of pages in original Judgment: 04

Case Note:

Service - Punishment - Authority to pass - Regulation 5(3) of Discipline and Appeal Regulations, 1976 - Respondent was appointed on post of Clerk with Appellant-Bank - He was put under suspension in view of order passed by Deputy General Manager of Bank - Inquiring Officer submitted his report holding Respondent guilty of charges - Thereafter, order was passed by General Manager whereby punishment of compulsory retirement was inflicted upon Respondent - Appeal preferred by Respondent was dismissed by Appellate Authority - Respondent challenged said order by filing writ petition before High Court - Single Judge came to conclusion that the General Manager of Bank was justified in passing order in view of Regulation 5(3) of Regulations - Bank has challenged this order before Division Bench - Division Bench had set aside order of Single Judge and remitted matter to Deputy General Manager - Hence, present appeal - Whether Division Bench erred in holding that General manager had no authority to pass order of punishment.

Brief Facts:

The Respondent was appointed on the post of Clerk with the Appellant-Bank. He was put under suspension in view of the order passed by the Deputy General Manager of the Bank in contemplation of a departmental proceedings. On the basis of the materials on record, the Inquiring Officer submitted his report holding the Respondent guilty of the charges. A copy of the inquiry report was forwarded to the Respondent by letter issued under the signature of the Deputy General Manager and Disciplinary Authority. The Respondent was called upon to file his representation or submissions on the findings arrived at by the Inquiring Authority. Accordingly, the Respondent submitted his representation/submissions. Thereafter, an order was passed by the General Manager and Disciplinary Authority, whereby the punishment of compulsory retirement was inflicted upon the Respondent. The appeal preferred by the Respondent was dismissed by the Appellate Authority. The Respondent challenged the said order by filing a writ petition before the High Court. Single Judge came to the conclusion that the General Manager of the Bank was justified in passing the order in view of Regulation 5(3) of the Discipline and Appeal Regulations, 1976. On appeal against sad order, Division Bench had set aside the order of the Single Judge and remitted the matter to the Deputy General Manager to proceed with the inquiry from the stage of receipt of the inquiry report and thereafter to conclude the proceeding in accordance with law.

Held, while allowing the appeal:

i. It was clear from the Regulation 5(3) that the Disciplinary Authority or any other authority higher than it, may impose any penalties specified in Regulation 4 on any officer employee. In the instant case, the departmental proceedings against the Respondent were initiated by the Deputy General Manager being the Disciplinary Authority. But the order of punishment had been passed by the General Manager, who was higher than the Disciplinary Authority. Having regard to Regulation 5(3), the Division Bench was not justified in holding that General manager had no authority to pass the order of punishment.

i. The order of the Division Bench impugned was set aside and the order of the Single Judge remitting the matter to the authorised Appellate

Authority for reconsideration of the appeal was restored.

CHAPTER SIX

Director General of Police, Railway Protection Force and Ors. Vs. Rajendra Kumar Dubey, 2020

Hon'ble Judges/Coram:
Dr. D.Y. Chandrachud, Indu Malhotra and K.M. Joseph, JJ.

Equivalent Citation: 2020(12)ADJ149, AIR2021SC91, 2021(1)ALLMR358, 2021(1)J.L.J.R.288, 2020(4)PLJR373, 2020(4)SCT716(SC), 2020(3)SLJ522(SC), 2021(1)SLR168(SC), (2021)1UPLBEC1, MANU/SC/0897/2020

Relevant sections: Rule153 of the Railway Protection Force Rules, 1987

Number of pages in original Judgment: 09

Case Note:

Service - Disciplinary Proceedings - Negligence in duty and abuse of authority - Rule 153 of the Railway Protection Force Rules, 1987-Punishment of Compulsory Retirement set aside - Reinstatement with consequential benefit, and 50% backwages directed -Whether order of reinstatement in such circumstances valid?

Facts:
The Respondent was appointed in 1984 as a Constable with the Railway Protection Force (R.P.F). He was placed under suspension pending enquiry. A charge sheet was issued for major penalty under Rule 153 of the Railway Protection Force Rules, 1987 alleging gross negligence in duty and abuse of authority. Disciplinary Authority imposed the punishment of removal from

service with immediate effect. The Appellate Authority in appeal reduced the punishment to that of reversion in rank for a period of 6 months without future effect. Later however, Respondent was issued a show cause notice under Rule 219.4 of the Railway Protection Force Rules proposing to impose the penalty of compulsory retirement from service. After considering his reply, the Authority held that the charges leveled against the employee were very serious in nature and proved beyond doubt. In view of the gravity of charges, the punishment of compulsory retirement from service with immediate effect was imposed. Appeal filed against this was rejected by Railway Board. High Court vide impugned judgment held absence of any pecuniary loss being caused, would not warrant the extreme punishment and accordingly quashed the Order ordering compulsory retirement. It was directed that the writ Petitioner be re-instated in service, and would be entitled to all consequential benefits, including backwages to the extent of 50% on the remitted post, without future effect. Hence, the present appeal by the department.

Held, while allowing the Appeal:

High Court must not act as an appellate authority, and re-appreciate the evidence led before the enquiry officer.

In the present case, there is no allegation of malafides against the disciplinary authority i.e. Chief Security Commissioner, or lack of competence of the disciplinary authority in passing the order of compulsory retirement, or of a breach of the principles of natural justice, or that the findings were based on no evidence.

A police officer in the Railway Protection Force is required to maintain a high standard of integrity in the discharge of his official functions. In this case, the charges proved against the Respondent "were of neglect of duty" which resulted in pecuniary loss to the Railways. The Respondent was a Sub-Inspector in the Railway Police discharging an office of trust and confidence which required absolute integrity. The High Court was therefore not justified in setting aside the order of compulsory retirement and directing re-instatement with consequential benefits, and payment of backwages.

The appeal is allowed, and the judgment of the High Court set aside and order of compulsory retirement restored. Appellant-Department directed to release Gratuity, if due and payable.

CHAPTER SEVEN

Arun Kumar Gupta Vs. State of Jharkhand and Ors., 2020

Hon'ble Judges/Coram:
L. Nageswara Rao and Deepak Gupta, JJ.

Equivalent Citation: AIR2020SC1175, 2020(2)ALT113, 2020(I)CLR(SC)919, 2020(2)J.L.J.R.82, 2020(2)PLJR82, (2020)13SCC355, 2020 (5) SCJ 609, 2020(3)SLJ40(SC), 2020(3)SLR945(SC), MANU/SC/0231/2020

Relevant sections: Section 327 of Indian Penal Code, 1860

Number of pages in original Judgment: 10

Ratio Decidendi:
A judicial officer's integrity must be of a higher order and even a single aberration is not permitted.

Case Note:

Service - Compulsory retirement - Present petitions had been filed by twp erstwhile judicial officers who were members of judicial service and were directed against orders whereby they had been compulsorily retired - Challenge was to orders of compulsory retirement and especially to reasons assigned or material ignored by Screening Committee of High Court - Whether impugned order of compulsorily retirement warrant any interference.

Facts:
The present writ petitions had been filed by two erstwhile judicial officers who were members of the judicial service and were directed against the orders whereby they had been compulsorily retired. The main contentions raised on behalf of the Petitioners were that their retirement was not in the public interest, their entire service record especially the contemporaneous

record had not been taken into consideration and also that the Petitioners have been granted various promotions which would have the effect of washing off their previous adverse entries, if any.

Held, while dismissing the petition:

i. As far as one petitioner was concerned, there were two very serious allegations against him. The first is that when he was working as Deputy Director, Administrative Training Institute, as many as ten ladies, who were Civil Service Probationers, made allegations that he was using unwarranted and objectionable language during his lectures, citing indecent examples and using words having double meaning, thereby causing embarrassment to the lady officers. This court had perused the complaints which are filed with the reply and the common refrain was that the language used by said petitioner during his lectures was highly sexist.
ii. There was also another allegation that he had physically hurt a washerman by placing a hot iron on the head of the washerman who had allegedly not ironed his clothes properly. It would be pertinent to mention that the Principal District Judge had reported to the High Court that the victim had personally approached him immediately after the occurrence and he (the Principal District Judge) found that the victim had sustained burn injuries and he got the victim treated. It was true that said petitioner was exonerated by the successor judicial officer before whom the complainant denied having suffered any injury but we may note that this is a preliminary inquiry and the successor Principal District Judge did not even care to examine his predecessor Principal District Judge, who had not only been approached personally by the washerman, but who had himself noted the burn injuries and had got the victim treated. Therefore, the Screening Committee was right that the victim may have been put under some pressure to withdraw his complaint. These occurrences could not be said to be very old.

i. As far as other petitioner was concerned, it was found that his record on many counts was not at all good. His reputation and integrity have been doubted more than once. Some adverse remarks had been conveyed to him. Even his knowledge of law and procedure was found to be average and his relation with the members of the Bar was found not very good. There were also allegations against him of having granted bail for illegal gratification and substance had been found in this allegation in the report of the Judicial Commissioner. The officer had granted bail by noting in the order that Section 327 of the Indian Penal Code, 1860 was bailable whereas the offence is non-bailable and an unrecorded warning regarding the integrity of the judicial officer was issued to him.

iv. The Senior judges of the High Court who were the members of the Screening Committee and Standing Committee had taken a considered and well-reasoned decision. Unless there were allegations of mala fides or the facts are so glaring that the decision of compulsory retirement was unsupportable this Court would not exercise its power of judicial review. In such matters the court on the judicial side must exercise restraint before setting aside the decision of such collective bodies comprising of senior High Court Judges.

CHAPTER EIGHT

Nisha Priya Bhatia Vs. Union of India (UOI) and Ors., 2020

Hon'ble Judges/Coram:
A.M. Khanwilkar and Dinesh Maheshwari, JJ.

Equivalent Citation: 2020(2)ESC406(SC), (2020)13SCC56, 2020(3)SCT455(SC), 2021(1)SLR800(SC), MANU/SC/0406/2020

Relevant sections: Rule135 of Research and Analysis Wing Rules, 1975

Number of pages in original Judgment: 35

Case Note:

Service - Compulsory retirement - Rule 135 of Research and Analysis Wing Rules, 1975 - Appellant joined Research and Analysis Wing as Directly Recruited under Research and Analysis Service (RAS) - Appellant filed complaint of sexual harassment against Secretary (R) -Incharge of Organisation and other person working as Joint Secretary in Organisation at that time - Departmental Complaints Committee concluded that no allegations of sexual harassment could be proved - Respondents declare Appellant as unemployable and declaration of unemployability of Appellant due to exposure as intelligence officer was made by way of order of compulsory retirement passed under Rule 135 of Rules - Appellant's challenge to this order was upheld by Tribunal and order of reinstatement of Appellant back in service was directed - Said order of Tribunal was impugned by Respondents before High Court - High Court upheld order of compulsory retirement issued under Rule 135 of Rules - Hence, present appeal - Whether impugned order of compulsory retirement issued under Rule 135 of Rules was sustainable.

Brief Facts:

The Appellant joined the Research and Analysis Wing as Directly Recruited under the Research and Analysis Service (RAS).The Appellant filed a complaint of sexual harassment against Secretary (R) -Incharge of the Organisation and person working as Joint Secretary in the Organisation at that time. The Appellant alleged that the charged officers subjected her to harassment by asking her to join the sex racket running inside the Organisation for securing quicker promotions and upon refusal to oblige, she was subjected to persecution. The departmental Complaints Committee, in its ex-parte report, concluded that no allegations of sexual harassment could be proved. The Respondents declare the Appellant as unemployable, having regard to the nature of work of the Organisation of which confidentiality and secrecy are inalienable elements. the declaration of unemployability of the Appellant due to exposure as an intelligence officer was made by way of an order of compulsory retirement passed under Rule 135 of the 1975 Rules. The Appellant took exception to this order before the Tribunal on the grounds of mala fides and manifest arbitrariness in the actions of the Respondents. The Appellant's challenge to this order was upheld by the Tribunal and order reinstatement of the Appellant back in service was directed. The said order of the Tribunal was impugned by the Respondents before the High Court, wherein the High Court, by an elaborate judgment, reversed the decision of the Tribunal and upheld the order of compulsory retirement issued under Rule 135.

Held, while disposing off the appeals:

i. The effect of any action taken under Rule 135 did not entail any penal consequence for the employee and, therefore, it could not be put at the same pedestal as an action of dismissal or removal, and no inquiry or opportunity of hearing as envisaged under Article 311 is required while taking an action under this Rule. Equally, it holds merit to note that mere loss of some future career prospects per se is no ground for invalidating an order of compulsory retirement as it may be in a given case an inevitable consequence of any such order. What needs to be delineated to attract the vice of invalidity to a statutory order was illegality, at least of a minimum standard to trigger the conscience of the Court. The exposition in Shyam Lal and Saubhagchand M. Doshi would squarely apply.

ii. The action under Rule 135 was not governed by Article 311 nor it offends the same-as these two provisions operate in separate spheres and thus an action taken under the impugned Rule (Rule 135 of the 1975 Rules) need not be preceded by the safeguards provided under Article 311 of the Constitution as such. Since the action under Rule 135 was exclusive and is invoked in the specified situations in public interest in reference to the Organization and at the highest level by the head of the Government, the question of violation of Article 14 on account of the denial of equal protection of law did not arise.

iii. It was noteworthy that in Indian constitutional jurisprudence, a duly enacted law cannot be struck down on the mere ground of vagueness unless such vagueness transcends in the realm of arbitrariness. However, challenge to Rule 135 on the ground of vagueness, could only be sustained if the Rule did not provide a person of ordinary intelligence with a reasonable opportunity to know the scope of the sphere in which the Rule would operate. In the present case, the test of reasonable man is to be applied from the point of view of a member working in the Organisation as an intelligence officer. The members working in the Organisation, more particularly a Class-I Intelligence Officer, ought to know the scope, specific context and import of the expressions-exposed as an intelligence officer, becoming unemployable in the Organisation or reason of security, as the case may be. A member working in the Organisation would certainly be aware of the transnational repercussions emerging from the exposure of the identity of an intelligence officer. Thus, there was no inherent vagueness or arbitrariness in the usage of above expressions so as to attach the vice of unconstitutionality to the Rule. However, whether or not an executive act of exercising the power under the Rule reeks of arbitrariness was a matter of separate examination, to be conducted on a case to case basis and did not call for a general declaration by the Court.

iv. The Appellant has not impleaded the concerned persons against whom allegations of mala fides were made, as party Respondent. Hence, those allegations could not be taken forward. Resultantly, the ground of mala fide action in fact did not survive for consideration.

v. The Appellant had not been able to establish the factum of non-application of mind in material terms and especially because the final decision had been taken at the highest level by the head of the Government in the aftermath of unfurling of successive events of exposure of Appellant to the public and media in particular. In other words, even accept the argument of personal animosity between the Appellant and the then Secretary, it did not help the Appellant's case as the final authority on the decision of compulsory retirement was vested in the PMO and there was no title of evidence regarding exercise of influence by the then Secretary (R) in the PMO. In an allegation of this nature, de-facto prejudice needs to be proved by evidence and this requirement of law fails to garner support from the factual position emanating in this case.

vi. The order of compulsory retirement in the present case was preceded by a chain of preliminary inquiry, in the highest echelons of the government and such preliminary inquiry, was advisable. For, it was only after a preliminary inquiry that the competent authority can satisfy itself about the existence of the prescribed ground in a particular case. However, the participation of the concerned officer in such inquiry is neither mandated by the jurisprudential essence of compulsory retirement or the rigid observance of the principles of natural justice. Such principles cannot be offered a free ride at the peril of larger public interests bordering on reasons of security of the Organisation or the State. Despite being harsh at times, unambiguous provisions of the Rule under consideration offer no space for infusing any element of judicial creativity against the legislative intent. It was held that Rule 135 of the 1975 Rules, excludes any requirement of prior notice or abiding by principles of natural justice.

vii. The officers, whose services were being terminated under Rule 135, ought to be provided with at least the extract of relevant applicable Rules alongwith the order of compulsory retirement so that the concerned employee would know about the entitlement and benefits under the governing Rule for pursuing claim there under in accordance with the law.

CHAPTER NINE

Ram Murti Yadav Vs. State of Uttar Pradesh and Ors., 2019

Hon'ble Judges/Coram:
Ashok Bhushan and Navin Sinha, JJ.

Equivalent Citation: AIR2020SC227, AIR2020SC227, 2020(3) ALJ 157, 2020 (139) ALR 603, 2020 2 AWC1908SC, 2020(1)BLJ396, [2020(166)FLR251], 2020(1)J.L.J.R.148, 2020LabIC799, 2020LabIC799, 2020(I)OLR72, 2020(1)PLJR94, 2019(17)SCALE639, (2020)1SCC801, (2020)1SCC(LS)245, 2020(1)SCT299(SC), 2020(1)SLJ560(SC), 2020(5)SLR781(SC), (2020)1WBLR(SC)606, MANU/SC/1710/2019

Relevant sections: Rule 56 (C) of the U.P. Fundamental Rules

Number of pages in original Judgment: 06

Ratio Decidendi:

A judge is the pillar of the entire justice system and the public has a right to demand virtually irreproachable conduct from anyone performing a judicial function.

Case Note:

Service - Compulsory retirement - Appellant while posted as Chief Judicial Magistrate granted acquittal to Accused in Criminal Case - Complaint was lodged against Appellant with regard to acquittal - Appellant was informed that on basis of enquiry, censure entry had been recorded in his character roll - Committee constituted for screening of judicial officers for compulsorily retirement under Rules recommended compulsory retirement of Appellant which was endorsed by Full Court leading to impugned order of compulsory retirement - Challenge laid out by Appellant to his order of retirement before High Court was unsuccessful - Hence, present appeal - Whether impugned order of compulsory retirement was sustainable.

Brief Facts:

The Appellant while posted as a Chief Judicial Magistrate granted acquittal to the Accused in Criminal Case. A complaint was lodged against the Appellant with regard to the acquittal. The Appellant was informed that on basis of the enquiry, a censure entry had been recorded in his character roll. The order of punishment was accepted by the Appellant without any challenge. A committee of three Judges constituted for screening of judicial officers for compulsorily retirement under the Rules recommended the compulsory retirement of the Appellant which was endorsed by the Full Court leading to the impugned order of compulsory retirement. The challenge laid out by the Appellant to his order of retirement before the High Court was unsuccessful.

Held, while dismissing the appeal:

i. The service records of the Appellant have been examined by the Screening Committee, the Full Court as also by the Division Bench of the High Court. The scope for judicial review of an order of compulsory retirement based on the subjective satisfaction of the employer was extremely narrow and restricted. Only if it was found to be based on arbitrary or capricious grounds, vitiated by malafides, overlooks relevant materials, could there be limited scope for interference. The court, in judicial review, could not sit in judgment over the same as an Appellate Authority. Principles of natural justice had no application in a case of compulsory retirement.
ii. The performance chart, as furnished by the Appellant, demonstrates that his assessment rates him as a fair or good officer only, except for one entry of very good. The submission that his integrity was certified on each occasion leaves us unimpressed. There could hardly be any direct evidence with regard to integrity as far as a judicial officer is concerned. It was more a matter of inference and perceptions based on the conduct of the officer.
iii. The complaint against the Appellant with regard to the acquittal granted by him was first considered by the Administrative Judge, who was satisfied that it was a matter for further enquiry. The comments of

the Appellant were called for. A vigilance enquiry was recommended by the Administrative Judge, who obviously was not satisfied with the explanation furnished. The officer holding the vigilance enquiry was also a judicial officer who opined that the act of acquittal by the Appellant was not above board. The comments of the Appellant were again called for. The Screening Committee consisting of three Judges, on an overall assessment of the Appellant's service record, recommended his compulsory retirement. The Full Court scrutinised the service records of the Appellant again while considering the recommendation of the Screening Committee and arrived at the conclusion that it was in public interest to compulsory retire the Appellant. It was undisputed that the punishment of censure meted out to the Appellant was never assailed by him.

A person entering the judicial service no doubt has career aspirations including promotions. An order of compulsory retirement undoubtedly affects the career aspirations. Having said so, we must also sound a caution that judicial service was not like any other service. A person discharging judicial duties acts on behalf of the State in discharge of its sovereign functions. Dispensation of justice is not only an onerous duty but has been considered as akin to discharge of a pious duty, and therefore, is a very serious matter. The standards of probity, conduct, integrity that may be relevant for discharge of duties by a careerist in another job cannot be the same for a judicial officer. A judge holds the office of a public trust. Impeccable integrity, unimpeachable independence with moral values embodied to the core are absolute imperatives which brooks no compromise. A judge is the pillar of the entire justice system and the public has a right to demand virtually irreproachable conduct from anyone performing a judicial function. Judges must strive for the highest standards of integrity in both their professional and personal lives.

CHAPTER TEN

Naresh Chandra Bhardwaj Vs. Bank of India and Ors., 2019

Hon'ble Judges/Coram:

Sanjay Kishan Kaul and Indira Banerjee, JJ.

Equivalent Citation: AIR2019SC2075, 2019(3)BLJ191, 2019(II)CLR612, 2019(2)ESC323(SC), [2019(162)FLR927], 2019(2)J.L.J.R.350, 2019LabIC2404, (2019)4MLJ637, 2019(2)PLJR363, 2019(6)SCALE553, (2019)15SCC786, 2019(2)SCT769(SC), 2019(6)SLR291(SC), MANU/SC/0576/2019

Relevant sections: Regulation 31 and 33 of Pension Regulations, 1995

Number of pages in original Judgment: 05

Case Note:

Service - Compulsory retirement - Penalty of - Appellant was employed with Respondent No. 1/Bank and sanctioned loans - Loans were ultimately classified as Non-Performing Assets and process of granting these loans was scrutinized by Bank, which were likely to cause loss to Bank - In pursuance of disciplinary proceedings, Appellant was visited with major penalty of removal from service - Contention of Appellant only with regard to quantum of penalty on ground that in similar cases punishment of compulsory retirement had been inflicted on two officers - Hence, present appeal - Whether penalty of compulsory retirement had been attracted in case of Appellant.

Brief Facts:

The Appellant was employed with Respondent No. 1/Bank and sanctioned loans. These loans were ultimately classified as Non-Performing Assets and the process of granting these loans was scrutinised by the Bank when various procedural abnormalities were found, which were likely to cause a loss to the Bank. In pursuance of the disciplinary proceedings initiated the Appellant was visited with the major penalty of removal from service which shall not be disqualification for future employment upon the Appellant. Contention of Appellant only with regard to the quantum of penalty on the ground that in similar cases punishment of compulsory retirement had been inflicted on two officers.

Held, while allowing the appeal:

i. A reading of the recommendations of the Chief Vigilance Officer shows that while earlier the proposal was for removal from service for all the three officers, in respect of other two officers it was converted into compulsory retirement while not doing so in the case of the Appellant. The rationale was stated to be the seriousness of the acts of misconduct of the Appellant and the fact that he was the recommending authority in two cases and the sanctioning authority in three other cases. However, the real reason comes out that while the other two officers were provident fund optees, the Appellant was a pension optee. It was, however, not explained in any of the pleadings as to what was the financial ramification in respect of the two options and as to whether the Appellant would get a greater financial benefit by reason of being a pension optee.

ii. It was fail to appreciate that once there was no financial difference and the role was practically identical, why the Respondents hesitated themselves to convert the punishment inflicted on the Appellant from one of removal from service which shall not be disqualification for future employment to compulsory retirement. The only aspect was the nature of punishment which appears to tar the Appellant more than the other two officers without any financial implication for the Respondent-Bank.

iii. Therefore, accept the plea of the Appellant to convert his punishment to one of compulsory retirement.

CHAPTER ELEVEN

The State of Jammu and Kashmir and Ors. Vs. Farid Ahmad Tak and Ors., 2019

Hon'ble Judges/Coram:
U.U. Lalit and Indu Malhotra, JJ.

Equivalent Citation: 2019(2)ESC427(SC), 2019(2)JKJ1[SC], 2019(7)SCALE290, (2019)7SCC278, (2019)2SCC(LS)305, 2019 (9) SCJ 186, 2019(2)SCT827(SC), MANU/SC/0656/2019

Relevant sections: Article 226(2) of Jammu and Kashmir Civil Services Regulations; Section 5(1) (d) read with Section 5(2) of Jammu and Kashmir Prevention of Corruption Act, 2006 and Section 120-B of Indian Penal Code

Number of pages in original Judgment: 07

Case Note:

Service - Compulsory retirement - Article 226(2) of Jammu and Kashmir Civil Services Regulations - Respondent was appointed as Junior Engineer, Power Development Department and stood promoted as Assistant Executive Engineer - FIR was registered against Respondent in respect of offences punishable under Section 5(1) (d) read with Section 5(2) of Jammu and Kashmir Prevention of Corruption Act, 2006 and under Section 120-B of Indian Penal Code - In exercise of power conferred under Article 226(2), order was passed compulsorily retiring Respondent from service - Respondent challenged said order by filing Writ Petition in High Court - Single Judge allowed writ petition and held that order compulsorily retiring Respondent was not sustainable - State being aggrieved, preferred Letters Patent Appeal which was dismissed by Division Bench of High Court - Hence, present appeal - Whether High Court erred in holding that impugned order of compulsorily retiring Respondent was not sustainable.

Brief Facts:

The Respondent was appointed as Junior Engineer, Power Development Department and with the passage of time stood promoted as Assistant Executive Engineer. FIR was registered against the Respondent in respect of offences punishable under Section 5(1) (d) read with Section 5(2) of Jammu and Kashmir Prevention of Corruption Act, 2006 and Under Section 120-B of the Ranbir Penal Code. In exercise of power conferred under Article 226(2), an order was passed compulsorily retiring the Respondent from service. The Respondent challenged the said order by filing a Writ Petition in the High Court. The Writ Petition was allowed by a Single Judge of the High Court. It was held by the Single Judge that the decision to compulsorily retire the Respondent was taken merely on the basis of registration of a First Information Report against the Respondent without taking into account the APRs of the Respondent. Further, the norms evolved by the State to arrive at a decision with regard to integrity of the Respondent were also not followed and as such, the order compulsorily retiring the Respondent was not sustainable. The State being aggrieved, preferred Letters Patent Appeal which was dismissed by a Division Bench of the High Court.

Held, while allowing the appeal:

i. It was true that the exercise of power under Article 226(2) of the Regulations by the very same Committee did not meet with the approval, and the Division Bench in certain cases did reject the plea of the State Government, and affirmed the orders passed by the Single Judge setting aside the orders of compulsory retirement. It was also true that in those matters Special Leave Petitions were dismissed summarily. This court, however, need not go into the matter as some striking features which emerge from three matters were that in all these three cases the concerned Respondent official was never caught red handed while accepting bribe. However, observations which are identical in all three matters indicate that the Division Bench considered the matters from that premise. The basic foundation was thus incorrect. The matter from the perspective of Clause (iv) of Article 226(2) of the Regulations was also not considered. The orders of sanction in all these three matters highlight the acts of commission and omission on part of the concerned

Respondents as a result of which there was wrongful loss to the State and public interest was compromised.

ii. The said two features were common in all these three matters. The basic premise, on the basis of which the matter was considered by the Division Bench was incorrect and secondly, the matter was also not considered from the perspective of Clause (iv) of Article 226(2). Therefore, set aside the judgments and orders under appeal passed by the Division Bench of the High Court. The matters are remitted to the Division Bench for fresh consideration. These Letters Patent Appeals stand restored to the file of the High Court which may now be dealt with afresh.

CHAPTER TWELVE

Punjab State Power Corpn. Ltd. and Ors. Vs. Hari Kishan Verma, 2015

Hon'ble Judges/Coram:

Dipak Misra and Prafulla C. Pant, JJ.

Equivalent Citation: 2015XI AD (S.C.) 428, AIR2015SC2426, 2015(4)ALLMR986, 2015LabIC2433, 2015(4)SCALE311, (2015)13SCC156, (2016)1SCC(LS)140, 2015(2)SCT592(SC), MANU/SC/0363/2015

Relevant sections: Regulation 5(4) of Punjab State Electricity Board (Punishment & Appeal) Regulation, 1971

Number of pages in original Judgment: 07

Case Note:

Service - Compulsory retirement - Validity thereof - Punjab State Electricity Board Service (Premature Retirement) Regulation, 1982 - High Court, after relying on order passed in case of R.K. Panjetha, eventually treated order of compulsory retirement to be stigmatic and quashed it - Hence, present appeal - Whether order passed by 1st Appellant-State Power Corporation compulsorily retiring Respondent was in accordance with Regulation was sustainable in law or was it vulnerable being ex facie stigmatic - Held, entire record can be scrutinized by employer to adjudge justification of continuance of employee after reaching particular age as contemplated in Regulation - On scrutiny of words used in order, there could be no quarrel over fact that previous misconduct and punishment visited to Respondent had been stated - Decision-making process of Committee had been reflected in order - It included disciplinary proceedings, personal records and reputation - Entire record had been scrutinized, valid punishments had been taken into consideration and Annual Confidential Reports had been critically scrutinized - Order dwelled totally in different realm than order passed in R.K. Panjetha's case - Impugned order set aside - Appeal allowed.

Brief Facts:

The factual score as depicted is that the Respondent joined the services of the PSEB as a lineman on 6.2.1969. He was promoted to the post of Junior Engineer on 4.12.1973 and while holding the post of Junior Engineer in a disciplinary proceeding he was censured on 29.2.1988. In the year 1992 another disciplinary proceeding was initiated against him and he was visited with the punishment of stoppage of two annual increments without cumulative effect Under Regulation 5(4) of Punjab State Electricity Board (Punishment & Appeal) Regulation, 1971. He was also visited with stoppage of two increments with cumulative effect on 5.8.1993 in another disciplinary proceeding.

As the factual matrix would unroll the Respondent attained the age of 55 years on 19.4.2003, his date of birth being 20.04.1948. A High Empowered Integrity Committee (HEIC) was set up for screening the case of Respondent for his retention in service beyond the age of 55 years. As per the Regulations his case was considered by HEIC on 17.02.2004 and the committee after taking note of entire service record, the disciplinary proceedings initiated against him and the punishment imposed, his inefficiency in service and the confidential reports from 1992-2003, recommended his case for premature retirement and accordingly an order dated 19.02.2004 was passed by the Chief Engineer.

Held, while allowing the petition:

In the present case, on an anxious and careful scrutiny of the words used in the order, there can be no quarrel over the fact that previous misconduct and the punishment visited to the Respondent have been stated. The decision-making process of the Committee has been reflected in the order. It includes the disciplinary proceedings, personal records and the reputation. The reputation here has insegregable nexus, as is seen, with his ACRs and poor performance. The use of words like "inefficiency" and "not fit" cannot be put on a pedestal to confer on them such status so that they convey the meaning of "stigmatic". It cannot be remotely so. On the contrary, the order in ***R.K. Panjetha*** (supra) was *ex facie* stigmatic. It is worth noting that the learned Single Judge has drawn a parity solely on the ground that the relationship between an employer and employee is common and the employer PSEB has passed the order on two different occasions in respect of two different employees. Their status is absolutely irrelevant for the purpose of determination of the controversy in question. It is the nature of order which will judge its character, namely, simpliciter or stigmatic. The learned Counsel for the Respondent has canvassed with immense enthusiasm that one of the punishment has been set aside. Be that as it may, in such a case it will not make any difference. It cannot be said there is non application of mind. The entire record has been scrutinized, valid punishments have been taken into consideration and the ACRs have been critically scrutinized. The order, according to us, dwells totally in a different realm than the order passed in ***R.K. Panjetha's*** case. The distinction is obvious and same has been obviously missed by the High Court, which makes its order fallacious.

Resultantly, the appeal is allowed and the order passed by the High Court in Civil Writ Petition No. 12902/2004 is set aside. The Respondent shall reap all the benefits of compulsory retirement and be paid all his dues, if not paid, within four weeks hence. There shall be no order as to costs

CHAPTER THIRTEEN

Shakti Kumar Gupta Vs. State of Jammu and Kashmir and Ors., 2015

Hon'ble Judges/Coram:

J.S. Khehar and R. Banumathi, JJ.

Equivalent Citation: AIR2016SC832, 2016(1)ESC70(SC), 2016(1)JKJ1[SC], 2016(1)SCALE174, (2016)15SCC399, 2016(1)SCT532(SC), 2016(2)SLJ6(SC), 2016(4)SLR185(SC), MANU/SC/1464/2015

Relevant sections: Rule 24 of Higher Judicial Service Rules, 2009

Number of pages in original Judgment: 11

Case Note:

Service - Compulsory and Premature retirement - Petitioner selected by Jammu and Kashmir Public Service Commission - Appointment to Kashmir Civil Service (Judicial) - While in cadre of District & Sessions Judge - Placed in Selection grade - Present controversy relates to compulsory retirement of Petitioner - Compulsory retirement regulated under provisions of Higher Judicial Service Rules, 2009 - Rule 24 pertains to subject of premature retirement - Criteria/norms for continuity in service after ages of 50,55 and 58 years - Adopted by Resolution of Full Court of High Court of Jammu & Kashmir - Issue of premature retirement of Petitioner came for consideration in 2013 - Annual confidential reports for years 2008 to 2012 to be considered - For 2009, Petitioner assessed as "Average" - No annual confidential report recorded after 2009 - Assessment of 2009 considered for years 2010, 2011 and 2012 - High Court arrived at conclusion - Work and conduct of Petitioner - "Average" - Order of premature retirement of Petitioner - Annual confidential report of 2009 under assail - Present

Appeal - Whether annual confidential report of 2009 should be treated as an assessment of the work and conduct of the Petitioner - Whether treating the work and conduct of the Petitioner as "Average" for the years 2010, 2011 and 2012 on the basis of the report for the year 2009 sustainable in law - Whether the premature retirement of the Petitioner was justified

Brief Facts:

i. The Petitioner was selected by the Jammu and Kashmir Public Service Commission for appointment to the Kashmir Civil Service (Judicial) on 5.1.1987. He joined as Munsif (-cum-Judicial Magistrate, First Class) and was thereafter promoted as a Subordinate Judge(-cum-Chief Judicial Magistrate) in 1996 and thereafter, as an ad hoc District & Sessions Judge in 2002. While in the cadre of District & Sessions Judge, he was placed in the selection grade in 2011.

ii. The present controversy pertains to the compulsory retirement of the Petitioner. Compulsory retirement is regulated under the provisions of Higher Judicial Service Rules, 2009. Rule 24 of the aforesaid rules pertains to the subject of premature retirement. As per this rule, it is open to the High Court to evaluate the record of a judicial officer, before he attains the ages of 50, 55 and 58 years, for ordering his premature retirement. In evaluating the record of the concerned judicial officer, the High Court is to follow the procedure for compulsory retirement under the service rules applicable to him. In the event of a judicial officer being found unfit to continue in service, it is open to the High Court to prematurely retire him, on attaining the ages of 50, 55 and 58 years.

iii. The criteria/norms for continuity in service after the ages of 50,55 and 58 years were adopted by a resolution of the Full Court of the High Court of Jammu and Kashmir in June 2013. The Resolution constituted the basis for determining the retain-ability of the Petitioner in service. In the Resolution, emphasis was placed on the immediately preceding five years record, to assess the potentiality and utility of the employee under consideration. Likewise, the Instruction postulated in addition to the consideration of the quality of his judgments, his institutional integrity in larger public interest, his judicial conduct, his administrative capacity, the rate of his disposal of cases, the character of the officer, the complaints, the enquiries and the vigilance reports lodged against him, his dealing with financial matters, and the like. Since the issue of premature retirement of the Petitioner came up for consideration in the year 2013, mainly the annual confidential reports for the years 2008 to 2012 were to be taken into consideration. In the summary, it is apparent, that for the period from 1.1.2008 to 31.12.2008, the Petitioner was assessed as "Very Good", whereas for the period 2.1.2009 to 31.12.2009, he was assessed as "Average". In terms of the Resolution, since no annual confidential report was recorded after the year 2009, assessment made for the previous year, i.e., for the year 2009 was taken into consideration as the assessment for the years 2010, 2011 and 2012. It is therefore, that the High Court arrived at the conclusion, that the work and conduct of the Petitioner was merely "Average", as his annual confidential report from the year 2009 to the year 2012 reflected him and having been graded as "Average". The annual confidential report for 2009 and the order of premature retirement of the Petitioner is under assail in the present appeals.

Held, while disposing of the petition:

i. It is not possible for this Court to accept the determination of the High Court, that the annual confidential report of 2009 should be treated as an assessment of the work and conduct of the Petitioner. The Court is satisfied in concluding, that no assessment whatsoever was made at the hands of the Administrative Judge, insofar as the above annual confidential report is concerned. The same was recorded, on the apparent grouse, that the Petitioner had not submitted his "self-assessment report". Even though, it was possible for the Administrative Judge to have filled up a number of columns based on the assessment of the judgments, and the record available to him otherwise, yet merely on account of the fact that the Petitioner had not submitted his "self-assessment report", the Administrative Judge recorded the "Average" report. The above report being not a truthful assessment of the various constituents of the judicial officer's work and conduct, it could certainly not be taken as an assessment of his work for the period from 2.1.2009 to 31.12.2009.
ii. It may be mentioned illustratively, that on the basis of the record accessible and available to the High Court, it was not at all difficult to evaluate the Petitioner (or for that matter any judicial officer) in respect of his knowledge of law and procedure, about impressions during inspection (how he conducts the Court, how he behaves with advocates

and litigants, his clarity and understanding of the submissions made at the bar, and whether he is able to dictate from the dias - at least miscellaneous orders), whether he is industrious and prompt in disposal of cases, whether he is an efficient judicial officer. Without any inputs which a judicial officer would provide in a "self-assessment report", the Administrative Judge can also record his views on the judicial officer's reputation for honesty, integrity and impartiality, and his assessment about the officers attitude towards his superiors, subordinates and colleague, as well as, behaviour toward members of the Bar and public, and also, areas on which the judicial officer had been counselled. The "self-assessment report" would also not be necessary, while expressing the judicial officers reputation in his private life or his character in his private life, or for that matter, the estimation of the judicial officer in the perception of members of the Bar and the public.

iii. It is therefore apparent, that most of the columns of the proforma prescribed for recording the annual confidential report, could have been filled up, without any difficulty, in absence of the "self-assessment report". The annual confidential report being bereft of any assessment of the work and conduct of the Petitioner for the period from 2.1.2009 to 31.12.2009, the same is liable to be treated as no report, for all intents and purposes. In view of the above conclusion, it is also imperative for this Court to further hold, that treating the work and conduct of the Petitioner as "Average" for the years 2010, 2011 and 2012 on the basis of the report for the year 2009 is therefore, also not sustainable in law.

iv. Insofar as the issue of premature retirement of the Petitioner is concerned, it is essential to notice, that the same was considered in the background of complaints made against him, by members of the Bar, more particularly, Advocates practicing in the District Consumer Forum, Srinagar, followed by another complaint, by the elected office bearers of the Bar Association, Srinagar, who had met the Chief Justice, specially in connection with their grievances and allegations against the Petitioner. There was also a complaint at the hands of one Shyam Lal. In furtherance of the complaint made by the aforesaid Shyam Lal, the Chief Justice of the Jammu and Kashmir High Court had directed the Registrar(Vigilance) of the Jammu and Kashmir High Court, to conduct a preliminary enquiry.

v. There were also other complaints which were shown to the Court, from the original record. One of the complaints was at the hands of Nissar

Ahamd Khan, who had alleged, that the Petitioner had required him to have his personal laptop of HP brand repaired. The complainant accordingly had got it repaired from "New A.S. Combines (Regd.)", an authorised HP service station, for which he had paid Rs. 6,500/-, which the Petitioner refused to reimburse. There were also complaints in respect of disproportionate assets held by the Petitioner. The Court did not verify the veracity of these complaints. The Court merely noticed that complaints were available in the record of the High Court, which could have been, and indeed must have been, taken into consideration, while taking the decision to prematurely retire the Petitioner.

vi. The decision to prematurely retire the Petitioner, came up for consideration before the Full Court on 3.6.2013. The minutes of the Full Court meeting have been placed on the record of this case, along with the supplementary affidavit filed by the Petitioner. A perusal thereof revealed, that the Administrative Committee of the High Court in its meeting held on 21/29.05.2013 had examined the past record, annual confidential reports, work done statements, and other relevant record/ material pertaining to the Petitioner, and had opined that he had lost his utility, and had become deadwood. The Administrative Committee accordingly recommended to the Full Court, that the Petitioner was not fit to continue as District and Sessions Judge, after the age of 55 years. Based on the aforesaid recommendation of the Administrative Committee, the Full Court discussed the matter on 3.6.2013, and arrived at its conclusion based on the service record of the officer.

vii. Based on his "Average" report for the year 2009, and in conjunction with the Full Court Resolution dated 3.6.2013, his annual confidential reports for the years 2009 to 2012 were also treated as "Average". As such, he was not considered suitable, to be continued in service. Since the Court already declared the annual confidential report for the year 2009, as no report in the eyes of law, and as such, nonest; none of the said reports of the Petitioner (of 2009, 2010, 2011 and 2012) could have been taken into consideration for the purpose of passing the order of premature retirement.

viii. It is apparent, that in addition to the annual confidential reports, it was concluded that the Petitioner was incorrigible, and that, it was not in public interest to continue him in service. It was also recorded, that credible complaints with regard to his judicial work were being received periodically. On the basis of the above consideration, it was felt that the officer had lost his utility, and had become deadwood. Based on the aforesaid determination, the Full Court accepted the recommendation of the Administrative Committee on 11.6.2013. The Full Court's decision to prematurely retire the Petitioner, was forwarded to the Government for approval. The Cabinet approved the recommendations made by the High Court. The Governor of the State of Jammu and Kashmir, also accorded his approval, to the premature retirement of the Petitioner. It is therefore, that the Petitioner was issued an order dated 24.1.2014, intimating him of his premature retirement on attaining the age of 55 years.

ix. Having given its thoughtful consideration, to the consideration of the Full Court, in respect of material other than the annual confidential report for the year 2009 (and of the years 2010 to 2012), the Court is of the view, that there was sufficient material justifying the premature retirement of the Petitioner in terms of Rule 24, specially when the same is read in conjunction with the Full Court resolution dated 3.6.2013. It may be noted that there cannot be concrete evidence in respect of allegations pertaining to integrity. If the competent authority arrives at a justifiable conclusion, on the basis of the record available in connection therewith, that itself would be sufficient to order the premature retirement of the concerned individual.

x. It is apparent, that based on the complaints received against the Petitioner, the Chief Justice of the High Court of Jammu and Kashmir, afforded him an audience on 11.09.2012. The Chief Justice counselled the Petitioner, with reference to the complaints received against him. Few of the complaints received against the Petitioner, have been referred to above. The complaints expressed aspersions on the Petitioner's financial dealings, and also, in respect of the Petitioner's conduct during court proceedings. The Petitioner's conduct was adversely commended upon by the members of the Bar of the District Consumer Forum, Srinagar, and by the Bar Association, Srinagar. A clear reflection that his behaviour with advocates and members of the Bar Association was improfessional and/or indiscreet. There were vigilance enquiries pending against the Petitioner.

xi. Besides all this, it is necessary to notice, that even though the Court had set aside the annual confidential report of the Petitioner for the year 2009, since it was based on the non-submission of the "self-assessment report" by the Petitioner, it is necessary to record, that the non-submission of the "self-assessment report" by the Petitioner, also reveals his behaviour and temperament. A perusal of the note of the Administrative Judge dated 29.5.2013 (extracted above) reveals, that the officer was adamant about not submitting the "self-assessment report". The stand of the Petitioner before this Court was, that the "self-assessment report", was to be furnished to the District Judge, who would then forward it to the Administrative Judge. This position adopted by the Petitioner cannot be accepted, in view of the clear instructions circulated by the High Court of Jammu and Kashmir, to all Additional District Judge Courts.

xii. In the above view of the matter, the Court is satisfied, that the determination recorded in the minutes of the Full Court on 3.6.2013 (even if the Court was to exclude the consideration based on the annual confidential report for the year 2009), were sufficient to justify the order of premature retirement of the Petitioner. The Court, therefore, upheld the order of premature retirement of the Petitioner dated 3.6.2013/ 24.1.2014.

xiii. During the course of hearing, the Court was informed by the learned Counsel for the Petitioner, that the retiral benefits of the Petitioner, had not yet been released to him. If the Petitioner has submitted all papers connected to his pension, the Court directed the High Court to process and pay the Petitioner all his retiral benefits within four months. In case, the Petitioner has not submitted his pension papers, he may do so within two weeks from today, in which eventuality, he shall be released all his retiral benefits, within four months from the date of submission of all his pension papers.

CHAPTER FOURTEEN

Rajesh Gupta Vs. State of J and K and Ors., 2013

Hon'ble Judges/Coram:

S.S. Nijjar and Anil R. Dave, JJ.

Equivalent Citation: 2013IV AD (S.C.) 478, AIR2013SC2130, 2013 2 AWC1808SC, 2014(2) CHN (SC) 123, JT2013(2)SC573, 2013LabIC1667, 2013(2)SCALE330, (2013)3SCC514, (2013)3SCC514, (2013)1SCC(LS)657, [2013]1SCR557, 2013(2)SCT185(SC), 2013(3)SLR11(SC), (2013)3WBLR(SC)60, 2014 (1) WLN 90 (SC), MANU/SC/0144/2013

Relevant sections: Articles 311(2) of Constitution of India

Number of pages in original Judgment: 09

Ratio Decidendi:

"Authority shall pass order of compulsory retirement of an employee on subjective satisfaction based on valid material present before it."

Case Note:

Constitution of India - Articles 311(2)--Employment--Compulsory retirement--Normally not punishment--But if it is stigmatic--It would be treated as order of punishment--Which cannot be passed in violation of Article 311(2) and rules of natural justice--Appellant compulsorily retired as Executive Engineer--But recommendation made by High Powered Committee therefore--Indubitably arbitrary--No material before said committee to conclude that officer possessed assets beyond his known source of income--In all annual performance reports, officer rated "very good", "excellent" and even "outstanding"--Order passed by State Government compulsorily retiring appellant--Suffering from vice of arbitrariness--Impugned order of compulsory retirement of appellant quashed--And appellant to be reinstated in service with 30% back wages but without any interest thereon.The order of compulsory retirement differs from an order of dismissal or removal both in its nature and consequence. However, in case it is found that the order is stigmatic it would be treated as an order of punishment, which cannot be passed without complying with the provisions of Article 311(2) of the Constitution and the rules of natural justice.

Brief Facts:

i. Upon being selected by the Jammu and Kashmir Public Service Commission, the Appellant was appointed as Soil Conservation Assistant in the Department of Agriculture Production in March, 1981. On 20th April, 1985 he was posted as Assistant Engineer in Rural Engineering Wing (hereinafter referred to as 'REW'), Ramban, District Doda, Jammu and Kashmir. He was promoted on the post of Assistant Executive Engineer in REW in September, 1988. While he was posted as such, three separate criminal cases were registered against him on the basis of (i) F.I.R. No. 49 of 1991, (ii) F.I.R. No. 63 of 1994 and (iii) F.I.R. No. 11 of 1995. It is not disputed before us that upon investigation in all the matters, the allegations made in all the three FIRs were found to be 'Not Proved'. In F.I.R. No. 11 of 1995, there was, however, a recommendation to initiate departmental action against the Appellant and some other officers. It is also not disputed before us, that no departmental action was ever taken against the Appellant. Record also does not show that any departmental action was taken against him. After completion of the investigation in F.I.R. No. 11 of 1995, the Appellant was, in fact, promoted to the post of Executive Engineer on 15.12.1996. In spite of having been promoted, the order of promotion was not given effect to. Therefore, the Appellant challenged the action of the Deputy Commissioner, Udhampur who had refused to give effect to the order of promotion by filing a writ petition in the High Court. The writ petition was allowed and thereafter the Appellant was permitted to join as Executive Engineer on 6th February, 2003. He worked as Executive Engineer at Jammu till 8th May, 2003. During this period, in the performance of his official duty, the Appellant was required to recommend the sanctioning of technical approval to the construction works of various projects.

ii. On 5th March, 2003, the Government of Jammu and Kashmir, General Administration Department by Government Order No. 306-GAD of

2003 dated 5th March, 2003 constituted a Committee to consider the cases of officers/officials for premature retirement in terms of Article 226(2) and 226(3) of the Jammu and Kashmir Civil Services Regulations, 1956. On 1st April, 2003, further directions were issued by the Government indicating the circumstances which would be relevant for making a recommendation for premature retirement of a public servant. On 9th May, 2003 the Appellant was directed to be attached to the office of the Director, Rural Development, Jammu pending an enquiry into some allegations on the Appellant. On 22nd July, 2003, an enquiry report was submitted into the suspected irregularities in the execution of "Rural Development Works" in the eleven Blocks of Jammu and Kashmir. Clause 1 of the terms of reference of the enquiry related to the execution of works during 2002-2003 particularly during the month of March, 2003. It was as under: Whether any irregularity has been committed in any blocks of District Jammu in the execution of works during the year 2002-2003 particularly during the month of March, 2003 in the matter of observing the coral formalities viz. issuing of technical sanction, approval of estimates and allotment of works to mates, test checks etc.

Held, :

i. This now takes us to the other material on the basis of which the recommendation has been made by the High Powered Committee. It has been noticed by us earlier that the Appellant was required, in the performance of his official duties, to recommend the sanctioning of technical approval to the construction of works of various projects. The allegation with regard to issuing back dated technical sanctions was duly inquired into. The conclusion ultimately reached by inquiry officer noticed in the earlier part of the order indicates that at best the Appellant acted in a casual and haphazard manner in the maintenance of records. Such negligence on the part of the Appellant cannot per se lead to the conclusion that the Appellant was acting in such a manner with an ulterior motive. The conclusions reached by the High Powered Committee also do not co-relate to the assessment of work and integrity of the Appellant in the annual performance report. As noticed earlier, in all the annual performance reports, the officer has been rated 'very good', 'excellent' and even 'outstanding'.

ii. In view of the aforesaid, the conclusion is inescapable, that the order passed by the State Government suffers from vice of arbitrariness. The High Court erred in arriving at conclusions which were not borne out by the record produced before the High court. In view of the settled law, it is not possible for us to uphold the judgments of the Single Judge as also of the Division Bench.

iii. Consequently, the appeal is allowed, the impugned order of the premature retirement of the Appellant dated 26th April, 2005 is quashed and set aside. It is brought to our notice that the Appellant has still not reached the age of superannuation. He is, therefore, directed to be reinstated in service. In view of the fact that the Appellant has not challenged the order of premature retirement on the ground that the action taken by the Government was mala fide, it would not be appropriate in this case, to follow the normal rule of grant of full backwages on reinstatement. We, however, direct that the Appellant shall be paid 30% of the backwages from the date of order of premature retirement till reinstatement. He shall not be entitled to any interest on the backwages.

iv. We may further observe that upon reinstatement, it shall be open to the Government to post the Appellant on a non sensitive post in view of the background of the case.

v. Let the order be implemented within a period of four weeks.

vi. There shall be no order as to costs.

CHAPTER FIFTEEN

Rajasthan State Road Transport Corporation and Ors. Vs. Babu Lal Jangir, 2013

Hon'ble Judges/Coram:

K.S. Panicker Radhakrishnan and A.K. Sikri, JJ.

Equivalent Citation: 2013X AD (S.C.) 306, AIR2014SC142, 2013 6 AWC6378SC, 2013(4)CDR830(SC), 2013(III)CLR602, [2013(139)FLR992], 2014(1)J.L.J.R.242, 2013LabIC4215, (2013)IVLLJ493SC, 2013(4)LLN1(SC), 2014(1)PLJR394, 2013(11)SCALE475, (2013)10SCC551, (2014)2SCC(LS)219, 2013(4)SCT438(SC), 2014(1)SLJ64(SC), 2014(1)SLR579(SC), MANU/SC/0940/2013

Relevant sections: Industrial Employment (Standing Orders) Act, 1946

Number of pages in original Judgment: 13

Ratio Decidendi:

"Power to retire compulsorily government servant in terms of service rule is absolute, provided Authority concerned forms a bonafide opinion that compulsory retirement is in public interest."

Case Note:

i. Employment - Compulsory retirement - Respondent/employee joined services of appellant/Corporation on post of driver on 14.2.1977--Screening Committee of appellant/Corporation constituted on 27.3.2002 to look into conduct and continuance of four employees who attained age of 50 years or had completed 25 years of service--Among these four persons, name of respondent/employee also appeared--Entire service record of respondent/employee gone into by Screening

Committee as well as Review Committee on basis of which decision was taken to retire respondent/employee prematurely--During period of 1978-1990 respondent/employee charge-sheeted in 19 cases--In few cases he was exonerated and in some other cases he was given minor penalty--Order of compulsory retirement cannot be set aside merely on ground that service record pertaining to period 1978-90 being old and stale could not be taken into consideration at all--Remote past of employee can be taken into consideration--Entire service record is relevant for deciding as to whether concerned Government servant needs to be eased out prematurely--Even service record after 1990 does not depict rosy picture--Nothing to show his performance became better during this period--Impugned order of High Court set aside--Order of compulsory retirement--Upheld. The High Court could not have set aside the order merely on the ground that service record pertaining to the period 1978-90 being old and stale could not be taken into consideration at all. As per the law laid down in the judgments cited, it is clear that entire service record is relevant for deciding as to whether the Government servant needs to be eased out prematurely. Of course, at the same time, subsequent record is also relevant, and immediate past record, preceding the date on which decision is to be taken would be of more value, qualitatively. What is to be examined is the "overall performance" on the basis of "entire service record" to come to the conclusion as to whether the concerned employee has become a deadwood and it is public interest to retire him compulsorily. The Authority must consider and examine the overall effect of the entries of the officer concerned and not an isolated entry, as it may well be in some cases that in spite of satisfactory performance, the Authority may desire to compulsorily retire an employee in public interest, as in the opinion of the said authority, the post has to be manned by a more efficient and dynamic person and if there is sufficient material on record to show that the employee "rendered himself a liability to the institution", there is no occasion for the Court to interfere in the exercise of its limited power of judicial review.

ii. Employment - Compulsory retirement--Judicial review--Scope of--Very limited--Interference of court with order of compulsory retirement permissible only on ground of non-application of mind, mala fide, perverse or arbitrary or if there is non-compliance of statutory duty by statutory authority.

iii. Employment - Compulsory retirement--Power to retire compulsorily, Government servant in terms of service rule is absolute, provided authority concerned forms bona fide opinion that compulsory retirement is in public interest.

Brief Facts:

i. Rajasthan State Road Transport Corporation is the Appellant in the instant petition through of which it impugns the validity of the orders dated 16.1.2013 passed by Division Bench of the High Court of Judicature For Rajasthan, Bench at Jaipur. The Division Bench has dismissed the Writ Appeal of the Appellant and confirmed the orders of the Additional Judge passed in the Writ Petition filed by the Respondent herein, quashing the orders of compulsory retirement of the Respondent with the direction that the Respondent would be deemed to be in the service as if the order of compulsory retirement had not been passed and as a consequence the Respondent is held entitled to all consequential benefits.

ii. The Respondent joined the services of the Appellant on the post of Driver on 14.2.1977. He was placed on probation for a period of one year.

iii. The Appellant has framed Standing Orders for its employees known as the Rajasthan State Road Transport Workers and workshop Employees Standing Orders, 1965 (hereinafter to be referred as the 'Standing Orders'). These orders are duly certified by the Authority under the provisions of Industrial Employment (Standing Orders) Act, 1946. Subsequently, there was an amendment in these Standing Orders and certain new clauses under Rule 18, were inserted introducing the provision of compulsory and voluntary retirement.

Held, while dismissing the appeal:

i. The principle of law which is clarified and stands crystallized after the judgment in *Pyare Mohan Lal v. State of Jharkhand and Ors.* MANU/SC/0696/2010 : 2010 (10) SCC 693 is that after the promotion of an employee the adverse entries prior thereto would have no relevance and can be treated as wiped off when the case of the government employee is to be considered for further promotion. However, this 'washed off theory' will have no application when case of an employee is being assessed to determine whether he is fit to be retained in service or requires to be given compulsory retirement. The rationale given is that since such an assessment is based on "entire service record", there is no question of not taking into consideration an earlier old adverse entries or record of the old period. We may hasten to add that while such a record can be taken into consideration, at the same time, the service record of the immediate past period will have to be given due credence and weightage. For example, as against some very old adverse entries where the immediate past record shows exemplary performance, ignoring such a record of recent past and acting only on the basis of old adverse entries, to retire a person will be a clear example of arbitrary exercise of power. However, if old record pertains to integrity of a person then that may be sufficient to justify the order of premature retirement of the government servant.

ii. Having taken note of the correct principles which need to be applied, we can safely conclude that the order of the High Court based solely on the judgment in the case of *Brij Mohan Singh Chopra* was not correct. The High Court could not have set aside the order merely on the ground that service record pertaining to the period 1978-90 being old and stale could not be taken into consideration at all. As per the law laid down in the aforesaid judgments, it is clear that entire service record is relevant for deciding as to whether the government servant needs to be eased out prematurely. of course, at the same time, subsequent record is also relevant, and immediate past record, preceding the date on which decision is to be taken would be of more value, qualitatively. What is to be examined is the "overall performance" on the basis of "entire service record" to come to the conclusion as to whether the concerned employee has become a deadwood and it is public interest to retire him compulsorily. The Authority must consider and examine the overall effect of the entries of the officer concerned and not an isolated entry, as it may well be in some cases that in spite of satisfactory performance, the Authority may desire to compulsorily retire an employee in public interest, as in the opinion of the said authority, the post has to be manned by a more efficient and dynamic person and if there is sufficient material on record to show that the employee "rendered himself a liability to the institution", there is no occasion for the Court to interfere in the exercise of its limited power of judicial review."

CHAPTER SIXTEEN

R.C. Chander Vs. High Court of M.P. and Ors., 2012

Hon'ble Judges/Coram:

R.M. Lodha and Anil R. Dave, JJ.

Equivalent Citation: AIR2012SC2962, 2012(5)ALLMR(SC)486, 2012(5)ALT17(SC), 2012 5 AWC4367SC, 2013(3)B.L.J.11, 2012(4)ESC555(SC), 2013(1)J.L.J.R.368, [2012(4)JCR170(SC)], 2012(3)JLJ245, JT2012(7)SC332, 2012LabIC4515, 2013(1)MhLj503, 2013(1)MhLJ503(SC), (2012)7MLJ78, 2012(III)MPJR287, 2013MPLJ261(SC), 2013(2)PLJR41, RLW2013(1)SC346, 2012(7)SCALE244, (2012)8SCC58, [2012]7SCR205, 2012(3)SLJ304(SC), 2012(5)SLR578(SC), 2012(4)WLN145, MANU/SC/0639/2012

Relevant sections: Rule 56(2)(a) of Fundamental Rules; Rule 14 of Madhya Pradesh Higher Judicial Service (Recruitment and Service Conditions) Rules, 1994; Rule42(1)(b) of Madhya Pradesh Civil Services (Pension) Rules, 1976; Rule1-A of Madhya Pradesh District and Sessions Judges (Death-cum-Retirement Benefits) Rules, 1964

Number of pages in original Judgment: 10

Case Note:

Service - Compulsory retirement - Rule 56(2)(a) of Fundamental Rules, as made applicable in State of Madhya Pradesh, Rule 14 of Madhya Pradesh Higher Judicial Service (Recruitment and Service Conditions) Rules, 1994, Rule42(1)(b) of Madhya Pradesh Civil Services (Pension) Rules, 1976 and Rule1-A of Madhya Pradesh District and Sessions Judges (Death-cum-Retirement Benefits) Rules, 1964 - Government passed order of compulsory retirement against Appellant in exercise of its power under mentioned Rules - Division Bench held that challenge to order of compulsory retirement of Appellant was ill-founded and set aside order of Single Judge whereby directed that Appellant be reinstated with all consequential benefits - Hence, this Appeal - Whether, recommendation made by High Court on basis of unanimous opinion to Government for compulsory retirement of Appellant and order of compulsory retirement issued by Government suffered from any legal flaw and whether, order of compulsory retirement arbitrary or irrational that justified interference in judicial review - Held, it was clear that Appellant did not have unblemished service record all along and he had been graded "Average" on quite few occasions and he was Assessed "Poor" in 1993 and 1994 - Further Appellant's quality of judgments and order was not found satisfactory on more than one occasion and his reputation was observed to be tainted on few occasions and his integrity was not always found to be above board - However material amply showed that material germane for taking decision by Full Court whether Appellant could be continued in judicial service or deserved to be retired compulsorily did exist - So it was not scope of judicial review to go into adequacy or sufficiency of such materials - Further Appellant's conduct had tarnished image of judiciary and he disentitled himself from continuation in judicial service on that count alone - Moreover Single Judge did not keep scope of judicial review in view while examining validity of order of compulsory retirement - Thus whole approach of Single Judge in consideration of matter was flawed and not legally proper - Therefore Division Bench of High Court was fully justified in setting aside order - Hence recommendation made by High Court to Government for compulsory retirement of Appellant and order of compulsory retirement issued by Government did not suffer from any legal flaw - Order of compulsory retirement was neither arbitrary nor irrational justifying any interference in judicial review - Appeal dismissed.

Brief Facts:

i. On 13.09.2004, the Appellant, who was working on the post of District and Sessions Judge, Punna was compulsorily retired from the service in the public interest by the Government of Madhya Pradesh (for short, 'the Government') on the request of the Madhya Pradesh High Court (for short, 'High Court'). The order of compulsory retirement was issued by the Government in exercise of its power under amended Rule 56(2)(a) of the Fundamental Rules, as made applicable in the State of Madhya Pradesh, Rule 14 of the Madhya Pradesh Higher Judicial Service (Recruitment and Service Conditions) Rules, 1994 (for short, '1994

Rules'), Rule 42(1)(b) of the Madhya Pradesh Civil Services (Pension) Rules, 1976 (for short, '1976 Rules') and Rule 1-A of Madhya Pradesh District and Sessions Judges (Death-cum-Retirement Benefits) Rules, 1964 (for short, '1964 Rules'). In lieu of notice of three months, it was directed in the order that the Appellant shall be entitled to three months' salary and allowances which he was receiving prior to his retirement.

ii. The Appellant challenged the above order of compulsory retirement by filing a writ petition before the High Court. The Single Judge of that Court by his order dated 20.04.2006, allowed the writ petition; quashed the order of compulsory retirement dated 13.09.2004 and directed that he be reinstated with all consequential benefits.

iii. The High Court on the administrative side challenged the order of Single Judge in writ appeal. The Division Bench of that Court on consideration of the entire matter held that the challenge to the order of compulsory retirement was ill-founded and, accordingly, set aside the order of the Single Judge vide its judgment dated 23.11.2006. It is from this order that the Appellant has preferred this appeal by special leave.

iv. The Appellant was selected in the higher judicial service of Madhya Pradesh by direct recruitment. He joined the judicial service as an Additional District Judge on 17.10.1979. On 26.06.1985, he was confirmed as a District Judge. The Appellant was awarded lower selection grade on 07.09.1990 with effect from 24.03.1989. He was awarded super time scale in May, 1999 and above super time scale in 2002. As noted above, by the order dated 13.09.2004, the Appellant was compulsorily retired in public interest.

Held, while dismissing the appeal:

i. Learned senior Counsel for the Appellant placed heavy reliance on a decision of this Court in *Nand Kumar Verma* MANU/SC/0175/2012 : (2012) 3 SCC 580. Having carefully considered *Nand Kumar Verma* MANU/SC/0175/2012 : (2012) 3 SCC 580, we find that the decision of this Court in *Nand Kumar Verma* MANU/SC/0175/2012 : (2012) 3 SCC 580 has no application on the facts of the present case. This is clear from para 36 (Pg. 591) of the Report which reads as follows:

The material on which the decision of the compulsory retirement was based, as extracted by the High Court in the impugned judgment, and material furnished by the Appellant would reflect that totality of relevant materials were not considered or completely ignored by the High Court. This leads to only one conclusion that the subjective satisfaction of the High Court was not based on the sufficient or relevant material. In this view of the matter, we cannot say that the service record of the Appellant was unsatisfactory which would warrant premature retirement from service. Therefore, there was no justification to retire the Appellant compulsorily from service.

i. *Nand Kumar Verma* MANU/SC/0175/2012 : (2012) 3 SCC 580, thus, turned on its own facts.
ii. In view of the above, we are satisfied that the recommendation made by the High Court to the Government for compulsory retirement of the Appellant and the order of compulsory retirement issued by the Government do not suffer from any legal flaw. The order of compulsory retirement is neither arbitrary nor irrational justifying any interference in judicial review. The impugned judgment of the Division Bench is not legally unsustainable warranting any interference by this Court in an appeal under Article 136 of the Constitution of India.
iii. Civil Appeal is, accordingly, dismissed with no order as to costs.

CHAPTER SEVENTEEN

Nand Kumar Verma Vs. State of Jharkhand and Ors., 2012

Hon'ble Judges/Coram:

H.L. Dattu and Anil R. Dave, JJ.

Equivalent Citation: 2012(3)ALLMR13, 2012(3)ALLMR(SC)13, 2012 2 AWC2026SC, (2012)4CALLT1(SC), 2012(5)CHN230, [2012(133)FLR13], 2012GLH(2)158, 2012(4)J.L.J.R.213, [2012(4)JCR129(SC)], 2012LabIC1546, (2012)5MLJ133(SC), 2012(4)PLJR126, 2012(2)SCALE663, (2012)3SCC592, (2012)3SCC580, 2012(3)SCT192(SC), 2012(2)SLJ6(SC), 2012(3)SLR151(SC), 2012(4)WLN132, MANU/SC/0175/2012

Relevant sections: Section 302 of the Indian Penal Code; Article 235 of the Constitution of India

Number of pages in original Judgment: 09

Case Note:

Service - Compulsory Retirement - Legality thereof - Appeal against order passed by High Court of Jharkhand whereby, High Court had sustained order of reversion and order of compulsory retirement passed against Appellant - Whether High Court was justified in passing order, in reverting Appellant from post of Chief Judicial Magistrate to rank of Munsif (Civil Judge, Junior Division) - Whether High Court was justified in passing order of compulsorily retiring Appellant from service in public interest - Held, having accepted explanations and having communicated same to Appellant, High Court could not have proceeded to pass order of initiating departmental proceedings and reverting Appellant from post of Chief Judicial Magistrate to post of Munsif - On General Principles, there could be only one enquiry in respect of a charge for a particular misconduct and that was also what rules usually provided - When a completed enquiry proceedings was set aside by a competent forum on a technical or on ground of procedural infirmity, fresh proceedings on same charges was permissible - There was no justification for conducting a second enquiry on very charges, which had been dropped earlier - Law permitted only disciplinary proceedings and not harassment - In circumstance, impugned order reverting Appellant to lower Sanction of amount towards purchase of postage and service stamps for use of Department, could not be sustained - Object of compulsory retirement from service was to weed out dead wood in order to maintain a high standard of efficiency and honesty and to keep judicial service unpolluted - There was very limited scope of judicial review of an order of premature retirement from service - When High Court took view that an order of compulsory retirement should be made against a member of Judicial Service, then adequacy or sufficiency of such materials could not be questioned, unless materials were absolutely irrelevant to purpose of compulsory retirement - When an order of compulsory retirement was challenged in a Court of law, then Court had right to examine whether some ground or material germane to issue exists or not - Formation of opinion for compulsory retirement was based on subjective satisfaction of concerned authority but such satisfaction must be based on a valid material - It was permissible for Courts to ascertain whether a valid material existed or otherwise, on which subjective satisfaction of administrative authority was based - Totality of relevant materials were not considered or completely ignored by High Court - Subjective satisfaction of High Court was not based on sufficient or relevant material - It could not be said that, service record of Appellant was unsatisfactory which would warrant premature retirement from service - Therefore, there was no justification to retire Appellant compulsorily from service - Greater importance was to be given to opinion or remarks made by immediate superior officer as to functioning of concerned judicial officer for purpose of his compulsory retirement - Immediate superior was better placed to observe, analyse, scrutinize from close quarters and then, to comment upon his working, overall efficiency, and reputation - High Court was not justified in sustaining orders passed by Full Court of same High Court - Orders passed by High Court were set aside - Appeal allowed

Brief Facts:

The Appellant was initially appointed as Munsif (now known as Civil Judge, Junior Division) in the Bihar Subordinate Judicial Service in the year 1975 and his services were confirmed as Munsif in the year 1980.

Subsequently, in the year 1986, he was promoted to the rank of Sub-Judge (Civil Judge, Senior Division) and confirmed on the same rank w.e.f. 19.01.1988. In the year 1987, the Appellant was made Sub-Judge-cum-Addl. Chief Judicial Magistrate. Thereafter, in November 1989, he was posted as Chief Judicial Magistrate by the Patna High Court vide Notification dated 5.11.1989. While he was working as a Chief Judicial Magistrate at Gopalganj, an inspection was made by the portfolio Judge and on noticing certain omissions and commissions in granting bail in certain cases by the Appellant, certain adverse remarks were made against him in the note made on 09.03.1994. Further, the Appellant had also passed an Order dated 10.2.1994 granting bail to one person accused of offences punishable under Section 302 of the I.P.C. in Mohammadpur Police Station case No. 90/93. This was taken as an exception by the learned District Judge and also by the High Court while deciding the Criminal Miscellaneous Petition No. 11327/1994. The High Court of Patna vide Order dated 12.09.1994 in Cr. Misc. No. 11327 of 1994, whilst commenting adversely against the Appellant, had observed that the Appellant had granted bail in the said matter on extraneous consideration and further directed the matter to be placed before the Hon'ble Chief Justice of the High Court for taking necessary action.

Held, while allowing the appeal:

i. Ordinarily, the Court does not interfere with the judgment of the relevant authority on the point whether it is in the public interest to compulsorily retire a government servant. And we have been even more reluctant to reach the conclusion we have, when the impugned order of compulsory retirement was made on the recommendation of the High Court itself. But on the material before us we are unable to reconcile the apparent contradiction that although for the purpose of crossing the second efficiency bar the Appellant was considered to have worked with distinct ability and with integrity beyond question, yet within a few months thereafter he was found so unfit as to deserve compulsory retirement. The entries in between in the records pertaining to the Appellant need to be examined and appraised in that context. There is no evidence to show that suddenly there was such deterioration in the quality of the Appellant's work or integrity that he deserved to be compulsorily retired. For all these reasons, we are of opinion that the order of compulsory retirement should be quashed. The Appellant will be deemed to have continued in service on the date of the impugned order.

ii. Moreover, the District and Sessions Judge have the opportunity to watch the functioning of the Appellant from close quarters, who have reported favourably regarding the Appellant's overall performance except about his disposal, in the Appellant's recent ACR for the year 1997-98 and 1998-99. In view of this, the greater importance is to be given to the opinion or remarks made by the immediate superior officer as to the functioning of the concerned judicial officer for the purpose of his compulsory retirement. The immediate superior is better placed to observe, analyse, scrutinize from close quarters and then, to comment upon his working, overall efficiency, and reputation. In Nawal Singh v. State of U.P. MANU/SC/0756/2003 : (2003) 8 SCC 117, this Court has observed thus: In the present-day system, reliance is required to be placed on the opinion of the higher officer who had the opportunity to watch the performance of the officer concerned from close quarters and formation of his opinion with regard to the overall reputation enjoyed by the officer concerned would be the basis.

iii. In view of the above discussion, we are of the opinion that the High Court was not justified in sustaining the orders passed by the Full Court of the same High Court. Accordingly, we allow this appeal, set aside the orders passed by the High Court. Since the Appellant has retired from service on attaining the age of superannuation, he is entitled to all the monetary benefits from the date of his notional posting as C.J.M. till his notional retirement from service on attaining the age of superannuation, as expeditiously as possible, at any rate, within four months from the date of receipt of a copy of this order. Ordered accordingly.

CHAPTER EIGHTEEN

Rajendra Singh Verma (Dead) through L.Rs Vs. Governor of NCT of Delhi and Ors., 2011

Hon'ble Judges/Coram:

J.M. Panchal and H.L. Gokhale, JJ.

Equivalent Citation: 2011(II)CLR(SC)798, JT2011(10)SC304, 2011 (4) KLT(SN) 29, 2012LabIC3217, 2011(10)SCALE315, (2011)10SCC1, [2011]12SCR496, 2012(1)SCT43(SC), 2011(8)SLR452(SC), 2011(5)UJ3496, MANU/SC/1071/2011

Relevant sections: Rule 56 (j) of the Fundamental Rules, read with Rule 33 of the Delhi Judicial Service Rules 1970; Rule 16(3) of All India Service (Death-cum-Retirement Benefit) Rules 1958 read with Rule 27 of the Delhi Higher Judicial Service Rules 1970

Number of pages in original Judgment: 48

Ratio Decidendi:

"If the authority bona fide forms an opinion that the integrity of a particular officer is doubtful, the correctness of that opinion cannot be challenged before Courts."

Case Note:

Service - Compulsory retirement - Doubtful integrity - Delhi Higher Judicial Service Rules 1970 - Petitioners were compulsorily retired from service due to poor judicial performance and doubtful integrity - Hence, Present petition - Whether passing the order of compulsory retirement was justified - Held, if the Authority bona fide forms an opinion that the integrity of a particular officer is doubtful and it is in public interest to compulsorily retire them, it cannot be challenged before the Courts - Any judicial review thereon has to be made with great care and circumspection - When the Order of compulsory retirement is passed, the authority concerned has to take into consideration the whole service record of the officer concerned which would include non communicated adverse remarks also - Evaluation of the service record of the Appellants was neither arbitrary nor capricious or so irrational so as to shock the conscience of the Court to justify any interference - In cases of such assessment, evaluation and formulation of opinions, a vast range of multiple factors play a vital and important role and no one factor should be allowed to be blown out of proportion either to decry or deify an issue to be resolved or claims sought to be considered or asserted. Hence, Appeal was dismissed.

Brief Facts:

These appeals, by the grant of special leave, are directed against common judgment dated May 2, 2008 rendered by the Division Bench of the High Court of Delhi in C.W.P. No. 2157 of 2002, C.W.P. No. 1965 of 2002 and C.W.P. No. 2362 of 2002. The Appellants were the Members of Delhi Higher Judicial Service ('D.H.J.S.', for short). Mr. M.S. Rohilla and Mr. P.D. Gupta were compulsorily retired from service under Rule 56 (j) of the Fundamental Rules, read with Rule 33 of the Delhi Judicial Service Rules 1970, whereas deceased Mr. R.S. Verma was compulsorily retired from service under Rule 16(3) of All India Service (Death-cum-Retirement Benefit) Rules 1958 read with Rule 27 of the Delhi Higher Judicial Service Rules 1970, on different dates. They had challenged orders of their compulsory retirement from service by filing Writ Petitions under Article 226. Though the result of each appeal would depend on its own facts, having regard to the commonality of submissions on legal aspects, this Court had tagged these cases together and heard them one after the other. This Court proposes to dispose of the three appeals, by this common judgment for the sake of avoiding repetitiveness of legal principles. However, the Court proposes to consider each case on its own merits.

Held, while dismissing the appeals:

On a careful consideration of the entire material, it must be held that the evaluation made by the Committee/Full Court, forming their unanimous opinion, is neither so arbitrary nor capricious nor can be said to be so irrational, so as to shock the conscience of this Court to warrant or justify any interference. In cases of such assessment, evaluation and formulation of opinions, a vast range of multiple factors play a vital and important role and No. one factor should be allowed to be blown out of proportion either to decry or deify an issue to be resolved or claims sought to be considered or asserted. In the very nature of things, it would be difficult, nearing almost an impossibility to subject such exercise undertaken by the Full Court, to judicial review except in an extraordinary case when the Court is convinced that some real injustice, which ought not to have taken place, has really happened and not merely because there could be another possible view or someone has some grievance about the exercise undertaken by the Committee/Full Court. Viewed thus, and considered in the background of the factual details and materials on record, there is absolutely No. need or justification for this Court to interfere with the impugned proceedings. Therefore, the three appeals fail and are dismissed. Having regard to the facts of the case, there shall be No. order as to costs.

CHAPTER NINETEEN

Pyare Mohan Lal Vs. State of Jharkhand and Ors., 2010

Hon'ble Judges/Coram:

J.M. Panchal, Deepak Verma and B.S. Chauhan, JJ.

Equivalent Citation: AIR2010SC3753, 2010(6)ALLMR(SC)910, 2010(5)ALT49(SC), 2011(1)BLJ12, 2010(4)ESC590(SC), [2010(127)FLR402], JT2010(10)SC456, (2011)1MLJ143(SC), 2011(1)MPHT213, 2011(1)MPHT213(SC), RLW2011(1)SC321, 2010(9)SCALE528, (2010)10SCC693, (2011)1SCC(LS)550, [2010]11SCR216, 2010(4)SCT663(SC), 2011(1)SLJ71(SC), 2010(6)SLR4(SC), 2010(6)SLR4(SC), MANU/SC/0696/2010

Relevant sections: Rule 74(b)(ii) of Jharkhand Civil Services Code;

Number of pages in original Judgment: 09

Ratio Decidendi:

"Nature of judicial service cannot afford to suffer continuance in service of persons of doubtful integrity or who have lost their utility."

Case Note:

Service - Compulsory retirement - Rule 74(b)(ii) of Jharkhand Civil Services Code - High Court recommended compulsory retirement of six judicial officers including Petitioner - However, Respondent No. 2 issued a consequential order of compulsory retirement of Petitioner in public interest, invoking provisions of Rule 74(b)(ii) of Code - Hence, this Petition - Whether, Petitioner was fit to be retained in service or requires to be given compulsory retirement - Held, it was evident from service record of Petitioner that he had not been promoted in regular cadre of District Judge as he was not found fit for same because of adverse entries - Petitioner had made a bald assertion that adverse entries had not yet been communicated to him - More so, a single adverse entry regarding integrity of an officer even in remote past was sufficient to award compulsory retirement - Decision was taken by Full Court after due deliberation on matter - Therefore, there was hardly any chance to made allegations of non-application of mind or mala fide - Hence, Order passed by High Court was right - Petition dismissed.

Brief Facts:

Facts and circumstances giving rise to this case are that the petitioner was selected in the Bihar Civil Services (Judicial Branch) in 1982 and was appointed to the post of Munsif by the State and was confirmed in the grade of Munsif vide order dated 11th March, 1987. He was further promoted to the junior selection grade post in the cadre of Munsif of the Bihar Judicial Service vide order dated 23rd September, 1994. The Patna High Court issued Notification dated 10th March, 2001 promoting the petitioner to the post of Subordinate Judge.

Consequent to the bifurcation of the State of Bihar and formation of the State of Jharkhand, the services of the petitioner were allocated to the Jharkhand State by the order of the Ministry of Personnel, Public Grievances and Pension (Department of Personnel and Training), New Delhi dated 28th March, 2001. The petitioner was appointed as a Sub-Judge, Ranchi, vide Notification dated 21st April, 2001, issued by the High Court of Jharkhand and, subsequently, the petitioner was placed at the disposal of the State of Jharkhand as Under Secretary-cum-Deputy Legal Remembrancer and Law Officer in the Law Department vide order dated 1st August, 2001.

Held, while dismissing the petition:

Placing reliance on the judgments of this Court in M.S. Bindra (supra) and Baldev Raj Chadha v. Union of India and Ors. MANU/SC/0410/1980 : AIR 1981 SC 70, it has been canvassed on behalf of the petitioner that adverse entries had not been made in bona fide manner and as per the requirement prescribed by circulars etc. Therefore, the consequential order of compulsory retirement is illegal. There is no factual foundation on the basis of which such an assertion can be examined, nor there is a challenge in the writ petition to the said adverse entries. Petitioner sought quashing of order of compulsory retirement dated 20.5.2003 and not quashing of the adverse entries. Relief not specifically sought cannot be granted by the court. Therefore, there is no occasion for us to probe the issue further.

In view of the above, we do not find any cogent reason to interfere with the impugned order. The petition lacks merit and is accordingly dismissed.

No costs.

CHAPTER TWENTY

M.P. State Co-op. Dairy Fedn. Ltd. and Ors. Vs. Rajnesh Kumar Jamindar and Ors., 2009

Hon'ble Judges/Coram:

S.B. Sinha and A.K. Ganguly, JJ.

Equivalent Citation: 2009(2)ESC367(SC), [2009(121)FLR917], JT2009(6)SC263, 2009(IV)MPJR(SC)318, 2009(6)SCALE17, (2009)15SCC221, (2010)1SCC(LS)512, [2009]6SCR182, 2009(2)SCT571(SC), 2009(5)UJ2161, MANU/SC/0638/2009

Relevant sections: Article 12 of Constitution of India; Regulation 13 of Madhya Pradesh Cooperative Societies Act, 1960

Number of pages in original Judgment: 16

Ratio Decidendi:

"Whether an agency or instrumentality is State can be determined by applying the tests of administrative control, financial control and functional control.""If the relevant criteria, as has been laid down by the State, which has been adopted by the Federation, had not been acted upon, the Order must be held to have been suffering from jurisdictional error."

Case Note:

Constitution - Authority discharging public functions - State or not - Article 12 of Constitution of India - Madhya Pradesh Cooperative Societies Act, 1960 - Federation is a federal society registered under the Madhya Pradesh Co-operative Societies Act, 1960 - Regulation 13 made under the Act was amended with effect from 24th December, 2001 providing for compulsory retirement of an employee of the Federation on attaining the age of 50 years or completion of 20 years of service - Respondents were made to compulsory retire from service - Several Writ Petitions were filed by different employees of which some of them were allowed while some were dismissed - Single Judge granted 50 per cent back wages to 16 employees and Division bench did not interfere in the same but granted only 20 per cent back wages to other employees - Hence, present appeal by both the federation and the employees - Whether Madhya Pradesh State Co-operative Dairy Federation Limited is a "State" within the meaning of Article 12 - Held, whether an agency or instrumentality is State can be determined by applying the tests of administrative control, financial control and functional control - In the present case, Federation not only carries on commercial activities, but also it works for achieving the better economic development of a section of the people and seeks to achieve the principles laid down in Article 47 of the Constitution of India, viz. nutritional value and health - It undertakes a training and research work - Guidelines issued by it are binding on the societies - It monitors the functioning of the societies under it and is an apex body - Hence, Appellant would come within the purview of the definition of "State" as contained in Article 12 - Appeal by employees allowed and that of the Appellant dismissed Service - Compulsory Retirement - Relevant criteria - Arbitrariness - Scrutiny Committee constituted for scrutinizing the service records of the Respondents for about 20 years did not follow the relevant criteria fixed by the State through its circulars - Whether the Federation has acted arbitrarily by making the employees compulsory retire - Held, an authority discharging a public function must act fairly - Federation cannot take into consideration an irrelevant or extraneous matter which is not germane for the purpose for which the power is sought to be exercised - Scrutiny Committee as also the Review Committee was required to pose unto themselves a correct question of law so as to enable them to find out a correct answer - Criteria laid down in the circulars issued by the State of Madhya Pradesh should have been scrupulously followed - No material to show that the Respondents-employees had become dead wood, inefficient or corrupt, must be held to have abused its power - "Interest of the Federation" as contained in Regulation 13 of the Regulations would not mean that services of a large number of employees should be dispensed with only for the purpose of cutting administrative expenses - Yardstick has been fixed for the purpose of taking recourse to the power of compulsory retirement but there cannot be any doubt or dispute that such yardstick must be based on relevant criteria - If the relevant criteria, as has been laid down by the State, which has been adopted by the Federation, had not been acted upon, the Order must be held to have been suffering from jurisdictional error - Order of High Court does not suffer from any infirmity - Appeal by Employees allowed and that of the Appellant dismissed.

Brief Facts:

i. Before us, there are 52 matters. Out of 52 concerned employees, 16 Writ Petitions were allowed by a learned Single Judge. Writ appeals filed there against by the Federation were dismissed but only 50% back wages had been granted to the employees. Respondents have not questioned the correctness of the said judgment. Remaining 36 writ petitions were dismissed by a learned Single Judge. However, writ appeals filed there against have been allowed directing reinstatement of the concerned respondents with only 20% back wages.
ii. Federation is a society registered and incorporated under the provisions of the Madhya Pradesh Cooperative Societies Act, 1960 (for short "the Act"). It is an apex society classified as a Central Society. It is registered under Section 9 of the Act. The Government of Madhya Pradesh through its Veterinary Department had been carrying out in certain areas of the State activities of supply of milk through its offices established for the said purpose. A company known as Madhya Pradesh State Dairy Development Corporation Limited was incorporated on or about 22.03.1975 for carrying out the business of sale of milk and its products. It was registered under the Indian Companies Act, 1956. Its object was development and procurement of milk and for bringing out a 'white revolution'.

Held, while dismissing the petition:

i. Such a contention had not been raised before the Division Bench. It may be true that in a given case, this Court may allow the appellant to raise such a contention, as was done in the case of Kunal Singh v. Union of India and Anr. MANU/SC/0106/2003 : (2003)IILLJ735SC whereupon strong reliance has been placed, but it is not automatic.
ii. It is evident from the record that even before the learned Single Judge the said contention was not raised at the first instance. Only in the

review petition, the said contention was raised. But, the said review petition was dismissed. As indicated hereinbefore, the said contention was again not raised before the Division Bench. We, therefore, are not inclined to agree with the contention that in terms of the 1995 Act, the appellant should be given 100% back wages.

iii. For the reasons aforementioned, the appeals filed by the Federation are dismissed and that of the employees are allowed to the extent aforementioned with costs. Counsel's fee assessed at Rs. 10,000/- in each appeal.

CHAPTER TWENTY-ONE

State of U.P. and Ors. vs. Lalsa Ram, 2001

Hon'ble Judges/Coram:

G.B. Pattanaik and U.C. Banerjee, JJ.

Equivalent Citation: AIR2001SC1137, 2001(1)CGLJ424, [2001(89)FLR998], JT2001(3)SC242, 2001LabIC1100, (2001)IILLJ955SC, 2001(2)SCALE221, (2001)3SCC389, (2001)SCC(LS)593, [2001]2SCR108, 2001(3)SLJ111(SC), (2001)2UPLBEC1044, MANU/SC/0131/2001

Relevant sections: Rule 56, sub-rule (c) of the U.P. Fundamental Rules

Number of pages in original Judgment: 05

Case Note:

Service - compulsory retirement - petitioner compulsory retired from service on basis of report of Screening Committee - High Court set aside Order of compulsory retirement on ground that there had been no adverse entry in account of petitioner during last five years and sole entry of complaint cannot be basis for compulsory retirement - appeal - adverse entries did not stand extinguished by mere lapse of time - conduct of employee to justify conclusion of compulsory retirement is primarily for departmental authorities to decide - Court have no jurisdiction to interfere with exercise of power if arrived at bona fide on basis of material available on record - interference by Court in such matters in exercise of its jurisdiction is very limited - Order of High Court set aside.

Brief Facts:

i. The challenge in this appeal, by the grant of special leave, is to a judgment of the Allahabad High Court allowing a writ petition upon having an order of compulsory retirement dated 18th May 1998, set aside and quashed.

ii. Before adverting to the contentions raised in the matter, a brief factual reference would be convenient at this juncture. The petitioner was appointed as a direct recruit Naib Tehsildar on 19th May, 1955. The records depict that in April, 1980 the petitioner was promoted to the rank of Tehsildar and subsequently in March, 1995, to the rank of Deputy Collector. The petitioner joined the post as such in April, 1995 at Pitthorgarh District. Further in 1998, the petitioner however was served with an order of compulsory retirement in terms of the report of the Screening Committee dated 2nd January, 1998. The Screening Committee reported as below:

In the case of Sh. Lalsa Ram the Officer mentioned against S. No. 62 of the Enclosure A. The Screening Committee on considering thoroughly his relevant service records and the entries available in his character rolls, formed that Sh. Lalsa Ram was given adverse entry in 1967- 68 (from 14.4.67 to 21.9.67), in 1967-68 (27.9.67 to 31.3.68), 1981-82, 1982-83 and in 1991-92, and a particular adverse entry on 16.12.82 and censure entry on 18.8.86. Thus the service of Sh. Lalsa Ram constantly deteriorated.

i. Incidentally, the Screening Committee consisted of the Chief Secretary, Chairman Board of Revenue and Secretary Appointment Department - indeed a high- level Committee.
ii. It is on the report as above, the order of compulsory retirement dated 18th May, 1998 was passed and the High court has the following to observe in this regard:

"...On a close scrutiny we noticed that during the last five years' preceding action of compulsory retirement there has been no adverse entry in the account of the petitioner. The Screening Committee attempted to rely on the entries which related to the period of 1967-68 and some of the entries for the period of 1981-82. There is only one entry for the year 1991-92. This report otherwise records appreciation for the petitioner. But says further that some times there were complaints against the petitioner. The sole entry is not in close proximity and can not be the basis or foundation for the impugned action of compulsory retirement of the petitioner. The action, according to us, is without any basis and the same, therefore, can not be sustained."

Held, while allowing the appeal:

i. This Court on the basis as above in Gurdas Singh's case (supra) observed that is on this perspective the matter shall have to be considered as to whether it is in public interest to retain him in the service and the whole record of the service of the employee shall have to be considered including any uncommunicated adverse entry as well provided however, the service Conditions/Regulations do not run counter thereto. We also do record our concurrence therewith and record that the same holds good excepting however the issue of mala fides. The issue of mala fides has not been or even raised in the pleadings of the matter in issue and as such we are not called upon to delve into the same. The Appointing Authority upon consideration of the entire service record as required under the rules and having formed its opinion that the compulsory retirement of the respondent being in public interest issued the order and on the wake of the aforesaid, question of any interference of this Court does not and cannot arise. Interference in these matters by the courts in exercise of its jurisdiction under the constitutional mandate is very restricted and the courts shall have to tread on the issue with utmost care and caution by reason of very limited scope of interference. The High Court has in fact ignored this aspect of the matter and proceeded solely on the basis of the factum of there being no adverse entry in recent past. Needless to state that adverse entries did not stand extinguished by mere lapse of time but they continued to be on record and it is for the employer to act and rely thereon in the event of there being, a rule permitting an order of compulsory retirement.

ii. The High Court thus fell into an error and as such the order under appeal cannot thus to be sustained. The appeal therefore succeeds and is allowed. Order of the High Court stands set aside and quashed. There shall however be no order as to costs.

Videos & Tv Shows On Law & Exim

List of some important videos & TV shows on Law & EXIM by Adv. Jayprakash Somani on his YouTube Channel 'Jayprakash Somani EXIM & Legal'

Legal Videos: Hindi -English

1) SLP in Supreme Court / Special Leave Petitions in the Supreme Court of India

2) Transfer of Civil & Criminal Cases by the Supreme Court of India / Transfer of Matrimonial Cases

3) Appellate Jurisdiction of the Supreme Court of India

4) Jurisdictions of the Supreme Court of India

5) Public Interest Litigation in the Supreme Court of India / PIL in Supreme Court

6) Article 32 Writ Petitions in the Supreme Court of India

7) Bail Matters Top 10 Supreme Court Cases

8) FIR Quashing in High Court & Supreme Court

9) Bail & Anticipatory Bail Matters in Supreme Court

10) Insolvency & Bankruptcy Matters in the Supreme Court

11) Insolvency & Bankruptcy Code 2016 Part 1

12) Insolvency & Bankruptcy Code 2016 Part 2

13) Insolvency & Bankruptcy Code 2016 Part 3

14) Corporate Liquidation Process

15) Supreme Court Rules & Procedures Webinar of 2.5 hour on Zoom

16) RDDBFI Act, 1993 (Introduction)

17) The Indian Contact Act 1872

18) Negotiable Instruments Act (Introduction)

19) How to avoid matrimonial disputes& some more videos

20)SEBI Matters in the Supreme Court

21) Matrimonial Matters: Supreme Court's 20 Case Laws

22) Consumer Matters Supreme Court's 20 Case Laws

23) Service Matters Supreme Court's 20 Case Laws

24) How to Search Lawyer for Your Matter

25) Property Matters Supreme Court's 20 Case Laws

26) Bail Matters: Supreme Court's 20 Case Laws

27) Supreme Court / High Court Vacation Benches

28)69000 Teacher's Recruitment Matters of UP Government in the Supreme Court

29) Contempt of Court Matters in the Supreme Court

30) Advocate Act's Matters in the Supreme Court

31) Business Law Matters in the Supreme Court

32) Banking Matters in the Supreme Court

33) Labour Law Matters in the Supreme Court

34) Arbitration Matters in the Supreme Court

35) Careers in Law -Zoom Webinar by Adv. Jayprakash Somani

36) Civil Matters in the Supreme Court

37) Consumer Protection Act | Consumer Matters in the Supreme Court

38) Corporate Matters in the Supreme Court

39) Criminal Matters in the Supreme Court

40) Role of Respondent in the Supreme Court of India

41) Motor Vehicle Accident Matters in Supreme Court with case laws

42) Article 131 Original Suits in Supreme Court

43)PIL in Supreme Court/ Public Interest Litigations in the Supreme Court of India'

44)CAB Citizenship Amendment Bill is not Unconstitutional

45) Supreme Court of India Cases & Process – Marathi

46) Legal Services Export / Export of Legal Services

47) Transfer of Matrimonial Cases by the Supreme Court of India

48) Public Interest Litigation PIL

49) The Specific Relief Act (Introduction)

50) Corporate Insolvency Resolution Process CIRP

51)ABMM's Career 5 - Careers in Law

52) Transfer of cases by Supreme Court

53) Writ Petitions in High Court & Supreme Court of India

54) Supreme Court Jurisdictions - Appeals, SLP, Writ Petitions, Transfer, Original, Review, Curative

55)LEGAL INDIA TV Show: Cases Handled in Supreme Court

56) Corporate Liquidation Process

57) Legal Services Export / Export of Legal Services

EXIM Videos: Hindi -English

1) Yes, I can do Import Export Business Easily! 36 points excellent video in Hindi

2) Yes, I can do Import Export Business Easily! 36 points excellent video in English

3) Import Export Business – Hindi video

4) Import Export Business - English video

5) Export Import Marathi TV Interview

6) Scope for Commerce Students in International Business- TV Show

7) Scope for Management Student in International Business- TV Show

8) Scope for Engineering Students in International Business – TV Show

9) Women in International Business- TV Show

10) How to do Import Export Business Successfully!'

11) Where one can get full information on Import Export Business?

12) What to do import & export?

13) Import Export Workshop/ Training/Course/ Diploma

14) How to Start Import Export Business & How to grow it. Live Webinar

15) Success Stories & Failure Stories in Import & Export Business

16) For MSME Scope in Export & Import...

17) Exports In Agri. & Food Products – English & some more videos

18) Exports to Dubai, Aabudhabii. e. UAE

19) Jewelry Exports from India

20) How to attend EXIM workshop to become excellent Exporter

21) Import Export Best Training Course – Online & Offline

22) Agri Product Export

23) Scope for Woman in International Business

24) Management Graduates Scope in International Business

25) Pharma Product's Export

26) Best Import Export Course | Practical Training | Aaronica Global Exim

27) Import Export Business for Commerce Graduates

28) How Do I Get Export Orders? Finding International Buyers

29) What Is APEDA In Import Export Business?

30) Which Is The Best Product To Export From India?

31)EXIM Remark by Manoj Kumar Faridabad

32)EXIM Remarks by Mahesh Telangana

33) What Licenses I Need To Start Import/ Export?

34) How Can I Increase My Import Export Business?

35) Which Is Best B2B Website For Import/Export Business?

36) Export Import Management with Global Marketing

37) How to Start Export Import Business | 51 Points Video

38) Scope for Commerce & Other Graduates in International Business

39)BE A SUCCESSFUL EXPORTER FOR OUR NATION - Marathi video

40) Export of Textile , Cotton, Agri., Food, & other products & services

41) Exports from MP, CG, MH, GJ & CA in Fresh Fruits & Vegetables

42) Exports in Agri. & Food Products- Hindi

43) Start your Online/E-Commerce Business

44) How to Start Export Import Business & Grow it

45) Exports in Textile & Other Products

46) Start and grow EXIM business - Live English Webinar

47)'Import Export Business!' Why, Who, What &How can one do it easily!!

48) Live: Export of Product & Services During & After Lock Down Period

49) Frauds in Import Export Business

50) Import Export for Business Man

51) Import& Export for Women

51) Import& Export for Graduate & Post - Graduate Students

52) Agriculture Exports from India

53) Digital Marketing Setup - Marathi

54)2nd Secret of Successful Businessman

55) Digital Marketing Set up

56) Legal Services Export / Export of Legal Services

57) Export& Import with UAE

58) Service Exports / Exports by Service Providers

59) Import Export Workshop/ Training/Course/ Diploma

60) Exports& Imports with USA

61) Selection on Product for Export

62) Top Products Exported from India

63) What to do import & export?

64)ABMM Career 2 - 'Careers in Business & Industries

65) How to do Import Export Business Successfully!'

66)5 Secrets of Successful Businessman

67) Export from MP, Chhattisgarh &Vidarbha Nagpur

68)EXIM Hindi - Textile & Apparel Export

69)EXIM Hindi - Export Import Practical Training In Delhi, Kolkata, Mumbai and Pune

70) Import Export Business

71) Import Export Business Hindi

72) Import Export Business English video

73) Import Export Business Marathi

74) Women in International Business by Exim Guru Adv. Jayprakash Somani

75) Opportunities in Foreign Trade- Adv. Jayprakash Somani's special interview

List Of Adv. Jayprakash Somani's Books

1. Supreme Court of India's Leading Case Laws on 'Insolvency & Bankruptcy Code 2016'
2. Bail Matters – Supreme Court's Latest Leading Case Laws
3. Arbitration Matters- Supreme Court's Latest Leading Case Laws
4. Property Matters - Supreme Court's Latest Leading Case Laws
5. Matrimonial Matters- Supreme Court's Latest Leading Case Laws
6. Election Matters- Supreme Court's Latest Leading Case Laws
7.SEBI Matters- Supreme Court's Latest Leading Case Laws
8. Banking Matters- Supreme Court's Latest Leading Case Laws
9. Service Matters- Supreme Court's Latest Leading Case Laws
10. Contempt of Court Matters- Supreme Court's Latest Leading Case Laws
11. Consumer Protection Matters- Supreme Court's Latest Leading Case Laws
12. Corporate Law- Supreme Court's Latest Leading Case Laws
13. Supreme Court's AOR Exam- Leading Cases
14. Armed Force Tribunal - Supreme Court's Latest Leading Case Laws
15. Acquittal From 376 - Supreme Court's Latest Leading Case Laws
16. Negotiable instrument – Supreme Court's Latest Leading Case Laws
17. Contract Act- Supreme Court's Latest Leading Case Laws
18. Insider trading- Supreme Court's Latest Leading Case Laws
19. Foreign Exchange and Management Act- Supreme Court's Latest Leading Case Laws
20. Income Tax Act- Supreme Court's Latest Leading Case Laws
21. Company Law- Supreme Court's Latest Leading Case Laws
22. Competition & Monopoly Matters- Supreme Court's Latest Leading Case Laws
23. Compulsory Retirement- Service Matters- Supreme Court's Latest Leading Case Laws

These Books are available online at

1. **Notion Press:**https://notionpress.com/author/jayprakash_somani

2. **Amazon:**https://www.amazon.in/s?k=jayprakash+somani
3. **Flipkart:**https://www.flipkart.com/search?q=Jayprakash%20Somani

Printed by Libri Plureos GmbH in Hamburg,
Germany